Golf Essentials

FOR DUMMIES®

Golf Essentials

FOR
DUMMIES®

by Gary McCord
with John Huggan

COURAGE
BOOKS

AN IMPRINT OF RUNNING PRESS
PHILADELPHIA • LONDON

Published by arrangement with Hungry Minds, Inc. New York, New York, USA.

9   8   7   6   5   4   3   2   1
Digit on the right indicates the number of this printing

Library of Congress Cataloging-in-Publication Number 2001094406

ISBN 0-7624-1266-6

Designed by Matthew Goodman
Edited by Michael Washburn
Typography: Minion, Univers, and Cheltenham

This book may be ordered by mail from the publisher. Please include $2.50 for postage and handling.
But try your bookstore first!

Published by Courage Books, an imprint of
Running Press Book Publishers
125 South Twenty-second Street
Philadelphia, Pennsylvania 19103-4399

Visit us on the web!
www.runningpress.com

Icons used in this book

 Gary Says: Do this or I will never speak to you again.

 Golf Speak: Talk like this, and those golfers in plaid pants will understand you.

 Fore: "Duck! This is an awareness alert. Pay attention."

 Remember: This icons flags information that's important enough to repeat.

 Technical Stuff: This information will make your head spin; take two aspirin and get plenty of rest.

 Tip: This icon flags information that shows you really easy ways to improve your golf game.

Table of Contents

- -

Chapter 1

Chapter 2

Chapter 3

Chapter 4

Chapter 5

Chapter 1

•••••••

Getting into the Swing of Things

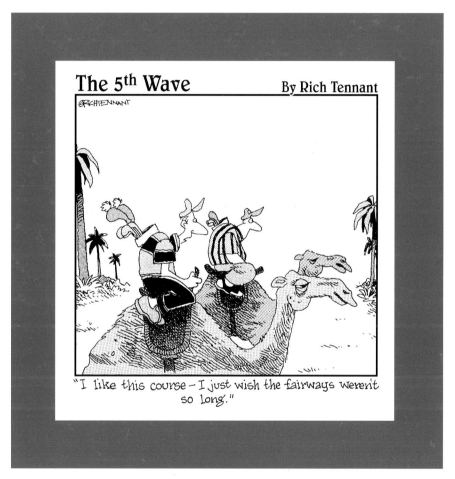

In This Chapter

••••••••••••••••••••••••••••

▸ Understanding the importance of good balance

▸ Types of golf swings

▸ Getting into position

▸ Mastering your swing

▸ Swinging from head to toe

••••••••••••••••••••••••••••

*W*hat is a golf swing? That's a very good question, one that has any number of different answers for any number of people. For most of us, a golf swing means "nonsequential body parts moving in an undignified manner."

In simple terms, though, a golf swing is a coordinated (hopefully), balanced movement of the whole body around a fixed pivot point. If done correctly, this motion swings an implement of destruction (the club) up, around, and down so as to hit a ball with an accelerating blow and with the utmost precision (on the center of the clubface).

I'm starting to feel dizzy. How about you?

The Importance of Maintaining Balance

The key to this whole swinging process is maintaining balance. You cannot hit the ball with consistency if at any time during your swing, you fall over. In contrast, when your swing consists of a simple pivot around a fixed point, the clubhead strikes the ball from the same downward path and somewhere near the center of the clubface every time. Bingo!

You're probably wondering where this fixed point in your body is. Well, it isn't your head. One great golf myth is that the head must remain perfectly still throughout the swing, which is very hard to do. I don't advise keeping your head still . . . unless your hat doesn't fit.

The fixed point in your golf swing should be between your collarbones and about 3 inches below them, as shown in Figure 1-1. You should turn and swing around that point. If you get that pivot point correct, your head will swivel a little bit as you turn back and then through on your shots. If your head appears to move like Linda Blair's did in The Exorcist, you've got it wrong.

Different Strokes for Different Folks

You can swing the golf club effectively in many ways. For example, you can have long swings and short swings. Imagine that you backed into a giant clock. Your head is just below the center of the clock. If at the top of your swing, your hands are at 9 o'clock and the clubhead is at 3 o'clock, you are in the standard position for the top of your backswing. The shaft is parallel to the ground.

Figure 1-1

At the top of John Daly's swing, which is a long swing, his hands are at 12 o'clock, and the clubhead is approaching 5 o'clock. Does your chiropractor have a toll-free number? Other swings have a shorter arc or circle. John Cook on the PGA Tour and Amy Alcott on the LPGA Tour, for example, have short swings. Their hands only get to 8 o'clock, and the clubhead gets to 1 o'clock.

Physical constraints dictate the fullness and length of your swing; the distance the club travels is unimportant.

Golf swings differ in other ways, too.

- ✔ Some players swing the club more around their bodies — like you would swing a baseball bat.

- ✔ Others place more emphasis on the role of their hands and arms in the generation of clubhead speed.

- ✔ Still others place that same emphasis on the turning of the body.

Physique and flexibility play a major role in how you swing a golf club. If you are short, you swing more around, or flatter, because your back is closer to perpendicular at address. (Address is the motionless position as you stand ready to hit the ball.) If you are tall, you must bend more from the waist at address, so your swing is automatically more upright. Remember, the left arm always swings about 90 degrees to the angle of the spine. Stand straight up and put your left arm straight out, away from your body. Now start bending at the waist. See how your arm lowers? It's staying 90 degrees to your back as you bend down. I wish I would have taken more geometry in school!

Factors of Flight

Although you can swing a golf club in many ways, in order to hit the ball squarely, all good swings have a few common denominators. But before I get to that, I want to break down the factors of flight:

- ✔ First, you want to hit the ball.

- ✔ Second, you want to get the ball up in the air and moving forward.

- ✔ Third, you want to hit the ball a long way.

- ✔ Fourth, you want to hit the ball a long way while your friends are watching.

- ✔ And last, you become obsessed, just like the rest of us.

Hitting the ball

You would think hitting the ball would be easy. But golf isn't tennis or baseball, where you can react to a moving ball. In golf, the ball just sits there and stares at you, beckoning you to make it go somewhere.

Here's your first thought: "I won't turn my body too much; I'll just hit the thing with my hands." That's natural — and wrong. You're worried about losing sight of the ball in your backswing and hitting nothing but air. You're not alone. We've all been through this sweat-drenched nightmare of flailing failure. Don't worry. You will evolve! You will make contact!

Getting the ball airborne

Okay, after a few fairly fruitless attempts, you're finally hitting more ball than air in your search for flight. You need a lesson in the aerodynamics of the game. The only time you want the golf ball to be on the ground is when you get close to the hole. To have any kind of fun the rest of the time, you want air under the ball; you need the ball to fly! Then you can stare with horrified fascination at the ridiculous places the ball ends up, which is the essence of the game.

One of my *Golf For Dummies* secrets is that the only time you should lift something is when you rearrange your living-room furniture. Never try to lift a golf ball with your club. You should hit down with every club except the driver and the putter, as shown in Figure 1-2. And when you do hit down, don't duck or lunge at the ball; hit down but keep your head up.

When you use your driver, the ball is set on a tee about an inch above the ground; if you hit down, the ball will fly off the top edge of the club. As a result, the shot will be high and short — not my favorite combination! With the driver, you want the clubhead coming into the ball from a horizontal path to slightly up when you make contact.

When you putt, you don't want the ball airborne. A putter is designed to roll the ball along the ground, not produce a high shot. So you need to foster more of a "horizontal hit" with that club. See Chapter 3 for information on putting.

If the club in your hands is a fairway wood or an iron, hit down.

Figure 1-2

Creating the power

As soon as the ball is in the air, your ego kicks in. Power with a capital P becomes your concern. Power intoxicates your mind. Power makes legends out of mere mortals. Power makes you want to get a tattoo. Power also sends the ball to the far corners of your little green world if you don't harness it properly.

Some professional golfers can create as much as 4 1/2 horsepower in their swings. That's some kind of giddy-up. This power comes from a blending of the body twisting around a slightly moving pivot point with a swinging of the arms and hands up and around on the backswing and then down and around in the forward swing. All of which occurs in the space of about one second!

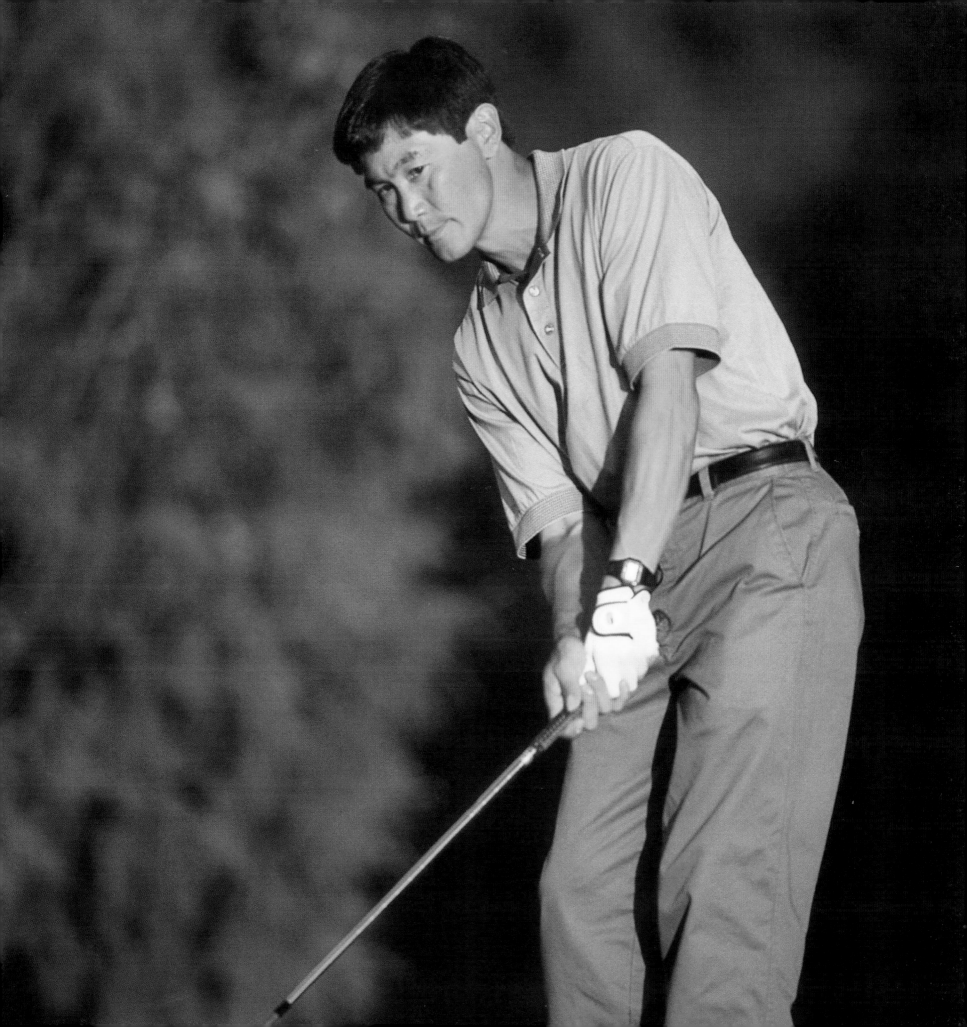

The key to gaining your optimum power is to try to turn your back to the target on your backswing, as shown in Figure 1-3. Which involves another *Golf For Dummies* must-do: On the backswing, turn your left shoulder under your chin until your shoulder is over your right foot. Make sure that you turn your shoulders far enough. Don't just raise your arms. Turning your shoulders ensures that you have power for the forward move. Turn for power. The unwinding of the hips and the shoulders on the downswing creates the power surge.

The same swing principles apply for women. However, to build momentum for the swing speed, ladies can rely on a longer backswing. A long backswing allows complete rotation in the left shoulder, which enables the left arm to extend fully and cocks the wrist to help release the power.

Figure 1-3

Turn your left shoulder "over" your right foot.

Building Your Swing

To become a golfer, you must master the building blocks of your swing. How do you hold on to the club so that you can give the ball a good whack? After you have a good grip, how do you align yourself to the target so that the ball goes somewhere close to where you aimed? What should your posture look like? How much knee flex should you have, and where in the world is the ball located in your stance? Should you look at the ball or somewhere near the sun? This section has the answers.

For natural left-handers, perfecting the golf swing can be tricky. In the past, there weren't many clubs designed for the lefty, and most course designs put left-handed golfers at a disadvantage. As a result, many lefties were taught to play right-handed. Today, however, technology has advanced to the point where some clubs are designed especially for left-handers.

Whether you swing left-handed or right-handed, it basically all comes down to which side has the stronger, most natural-feeling swing. To find out what works best for you, try swinging the club like a baseball bat from each side (keeping a safe distance from all breakable objects and small children). The muscles used in swinging a bat are similar to the range of motion in a golf swing. Of course, if you still have trouble hitting a straight shot, you can always blame the equipment. I do.

The grip

Although the way in which you place your hands on the club is one of the most important parts of your method, it is also one of the most boring. Few golfers who have played for any length of time pay much attention to hand placement. For one thing, your grip is hard to change after you get used to the way your hands feel on the club. For another, hand placement simply doesn't seem as important as the swing itself. That kind of neglect and laziness is why you see so many bad grips.

Get your grip correct and close to orthodox at the beginning of your golfing career. You can fake about anything, but a bad grip follows you to the grave.

Ladies tend to have smaller hands than men, so for them, it's important to have the right grip size on the club. Another tip for ladies is to use the closed-face grip position, which can help square the clubface during the swing.

Here's how to sleep well in eternity with the correct grip. Standing upright, let your arms hang naturally by your side. Get someone to place a club in your left hand. All you have to do is grab the club. Voilà! You've got your left-hand grip (see Figure 1-4).

Figure 1-4

Stand upright, letting your arms hang . . . and then grab the club.

Well, almost. The grip has three checkpoints:

1. First is the relationship between your left thumb and left index finger when placed on the shaft.

I like to see a gap of about three quarters of an inch between the thumb and index finger. To get that gap, you have to extend your thumb down the shaft a little. If extending your thumb proves too uncomfortable, pull your thumb in toward your hand. Three quarters of an inch is only a guide, so you have some leeway. But remember: The longer your thumb is down the shaft, the longer your swing. And the opposite is also true. Short thumb means short swing. (See Figure 1-5.)

Figure 1-5

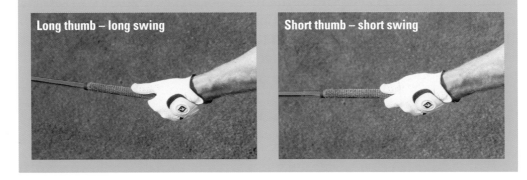

Long thumb – long swing   Short thumb – short swing

2. Check to see that the clubshaft runs across the base of your last three fingers and through the middle of your index finger, as shown in Figure 1-6.

This placement is important. If you grip the club too much in the palm, you hinder your ability to hinge your wrist and use your hands effectively in the swing. More of a finger grip makes cocking the wrist on the backswing, hitting the ball, and then recocking the wrist on the follow-through much easier. Just be sure that the "V" formed between your thumb and forefinger points toward your right ear.

3. Okay, your left hand is on the club. Complete your grip by placing your right hand on the club.

You can fit the right hand to the left by using one of three grips: the overlapping (or Vardon) grip, the interlocking grip, or the ten-finger grip.

Figure 1-6

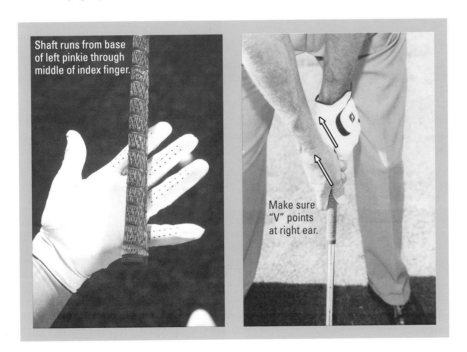

Figure 1-7

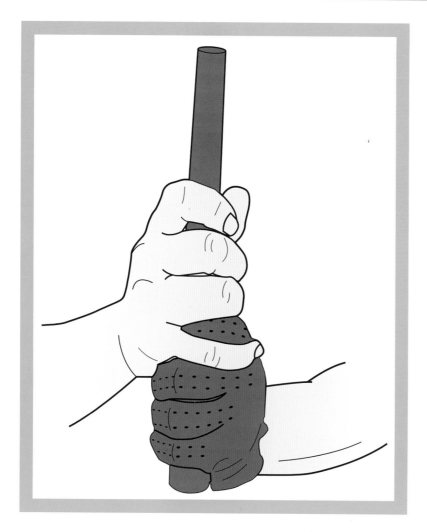

Vardon grip

The Vardon grip is the most popular grip, certainly among better players. The great British player Harry Vardon, who still holds the record for most British Open wins — six — popularized the grip around the turn of the century. Old Harry was the first to place the little finger of his right hand over the gap between the index and next finger of the left as a prelude to completing his grip, as shown in Figure 1-7. Harry was also the first to put his left thumb on top of the shaft. Previously, everybody had their left thumbs wrapped around the grip as if they were holding a baseball bat.

Try the Vardon grip. Close your right hand over the front of the shaft so that the V formed between your thumb and forefinger again points to your right ear. The fleshy pad at the base of your right thumb should fit snugly over your left thumb. The result should be a feeling of togetherness, your hands working as one, single unit.

This grip is very cool; probably 90 percent of Tour players use the Vardon grip.

Figure 1-8

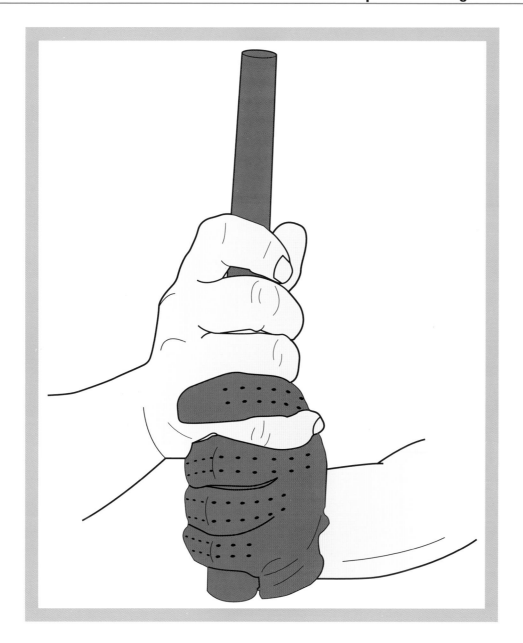

Interlocking grip

The interlocking grip is really a variation on the Vardon grip. The difference is that the little finger of your left hand and the index finger of the right actually hook together (see Figure 1-8). Everything else is the same. You may find this grip more comfortable if you have small hands. Tom Kite and Jack Nicklaus, possibly the game's greatest player ever, both use this grip for that reason. Many of the top women players use this grip, too.

Figure 1-9

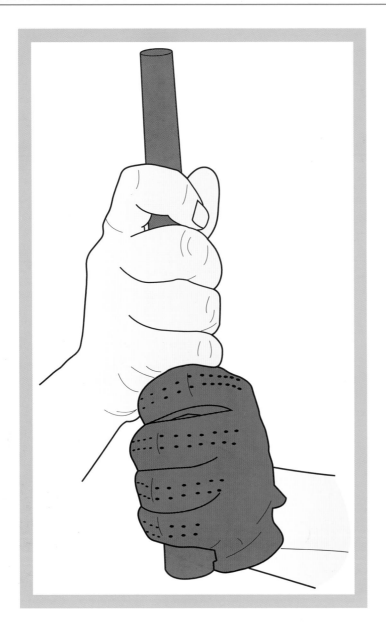

Ten-finger grip

The ten-finger grip used to be more common, but you still see it occasionally. PGA Tour player Dave Barr from Canada uses this grip. The ten-finger grip is what the name tells you it is. You have all ten fingers on the club. No overlapping or interlocking occurs; the little finger of the left hand and the index finger of the right barely touch (see Figure 1-9). If you have trouble generating enough clubhead speed to hit the ball as far as you would like, give this grip a try. Keep in mind that controlling the clubhead is more difficult with this grip because more "cocking" of the hands occurs.

Completing your grip

Put your right hand on the club, the palm directly opposite your left hand. Slide your right hand down the shaft until you can complete whatever grip you find most comfortable. Your right shoulder, right hip, and head lean to the right to accommodate the lowering of the right hand. Your right earlobe moves closer to your right shoulder.

Your grip pressure should never be tight. Your grip should be light. You should exert only as much pressure as you would when picking up an egg from a spotted owl. Lightly now! Spotted owls are becoming extinct!

Aiming

I played on the PGA Tour for 21 years, which means I took part in a lot of Pro-Ams. (In a Pro-Am, each professional is teamed with three or four amateurs.) And in every single one of those rounds, I saw someone misaligned at address. Sometimes that someone was me! Aiming properly is that difficult.

Generally speaking, right-handed golfers tend to aim to the right of the target. I don't see many of them aiming left — even slicers, whose shots commonly start left and finish right. Invariably, people tend to aim right and swing over the top on the way down to get the ball started left.

So what makes aiming so difficult? Human nature is part of it. Getting sloppy with your aim is easy to do when your mind is on other things. That's why discipline is important. Taking the time and trouble to get comfortable and confident in his alignment is one reason Jack Nicklaus was as great as he was. Watch him even now. He still works his way through the same aiming routine before every shot. And I emphasize routine. First he looks at the target from behind the ball. Then he picks out a spot about a couple of feet ahead of his ball on a line with that target. That spot is his intermediate target. Then he walks to the ball and sets the clubface behind it so that he's aiming at the intermediate point. Aligning the club with something that is 2 feet away is much easier than aiming at something 150 yards away.

How Nicklaus aims is exactly how you must work on your aim. Think of a railroad track. On one line is the ball and in the distance, the target. On the other line is your toes. Thus, your body is aligned parallel with but left of the target line. If you take nothing else away from this section on aiming, remember that phrase. Cut out Figure 1-10 and place it on the ceiling over your bed. Stare at it before you go to sleep.

Don't make the mistake that I see countless golfers making: aiming their feet at the target. If you aim your feet at the target, where is the clubface aligned? Well to the right of where you want the ball to go. This type of alignment will usually sabotage the flight of your ball.

Figure 1-10

Far too many golfers align their feet to the right of the target.

Aim the clubface where you want the ball to go. Your toe line should be parallel to your target line.

The stance

Okay, you're aimed at the target. But you're not finished with the feet yet. Right now, your feet are not pointing in any direction; you're just standing there. All the books tell you to turn your left toe out about 30 degrees. But what's 30 degrees? If you're like me, you have no clue what 30 degrees looks like or — more important — feels like, so think of 30 degrees this way:

We all know what a clock looks like, and we know what the big hand is and what the little hand does. If you are well versed in recognizing time pieces, you should be able to build a stance.

Your left foot should be pointed to 10 o'clock, and your right foot should be at 1 o'clock. However, this does not work during daylight saving time. You're on your own then.

Figure 1-11 demonstrates this stance. Keep it simple and always be on time.

Figure 1-11

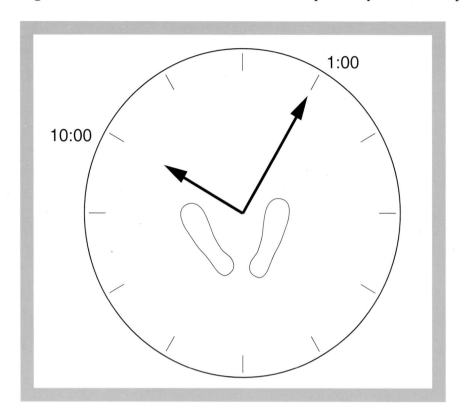

Width of stance is easy, too. Your heels should be shoulder-width apart, as shown in Figure 1-12. Not 14 inches, or 18 inches. Shoulder-width. Let the shape of your body dictate what is right for you.

Figure 1-12

With a driver, the gap between your knees should be shoulder width. Think "bow-legged."

Knee flex

Moving on up, the next stop is the knees. Again, you can read all sorts of books that tell you the precise angle at which your knees should be flexed at address. But that knowledge isn't going to do you much good when you're standing on the range without a protractor. What you need is a feel.

Think of your knee flex as a "ready" position. You've got to be set so that movement is possible. So, from an upright start, flex your knees and bend forward until your arms are hanging vertically, as shown in Figure 1-13. That's where you want to be. Just like a quarterback waiting for a snap. Or a soccer goalkeeper facing a shot. Or a shortstop ready for a ground ball. You're ready to move. Left. Right. Back. Forward. Whatever. You're ready. And remember, maintaining balance is the key.

Figure 1-13

Flex knees and bend forward until arms hang vertically.

Ball position

Where is the ball positioned between your feet? It should be positioned opposite your left armpit with a driver, which also should be opposite your left heel, and steadily moved back with each club until you get to the middle of your stance with a wedge (see Figure 1-14).

You are trying to hit up on the driver; that's why the ball is forward in your stance (toward the target). You hit down with all other clubs, which is why you move the ball back in your stance (away from the target) as the golf club increases with loft. When the ball is played back in your stance, hitting down is much easier.

Figure 1-14

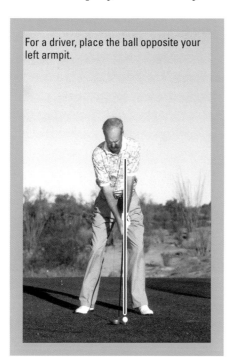

For a driver, place the ball opposite your left armpit.

The bottom of the swing

The bottom of the swing is an important yet frequently neglected aspect of golf. The bottom of the arc of the swing has to have a low point; hopefully, that low point is where your golf ball will be as you swing an iron. (Remember, the driver must be hit on the upswing.) If you don't know where the bottom of your swing is, how do you know where to put the ball in your stance? You can make the best swing in the world, but if the ball is too far back, you'll hit the top half of it. Too far forward is just as bad, and you'll hit the ground before the ball. Neither is too good an idea.

Fear not; such shots are not going to be part of your repertoire. Why? Because you're always going to know where the bottom of your swing is: directly below your head.

Think about it. I've already discussed how the ball is positioned opposite the left armpit for the driver. That position automatically puts your head "behind" the ball. In other words, the ball is nearer the target than your head. All of which means that you are going to strike the ball on a slightly upward blow. The bottom of the swing is behind the ball, so the clubhead will be moving up as it hits the ball, as shown in Figure 1-15. That's all right because the ball is off the ground perched on a tee. The only way to make solid contact (and maximize your distance) is to hit drives "on the up."

Figure 1-15

If it's on a tee, you better hit up or your club will go under.

The situation for an iron shot from the fairway differs from that of hitting a driver from the tee. Now the ball is sitting on the ground. Plus, the club you are using has more loft and is designed to give best results when the ball is struck just before the ground. So now your head should be over the ball at address and impact. In other words, something has to move.

That something is the ball. Start from the middle of your stance, which is where the ball should be when you are hitting a wedge, one of the shortest and most lofted clubs in your bag. Move the ball steadily forward — all the way to opposite your left armpit for the driver — as the club in your hands gets longer. (See Figure 1-16.)

So for me, the distance between my left armpit and chin is about 6 inches. With the driver, the ball is opposite my left armpit, and with the shorter irons, it's opposite my chin (that is, where my head is). In my case, the ball moves about 6 inches. Most golf courses are about 7,000 yards, so 6 inches shouldn't have much significance. Practice this part early in your development and then worry about the 7,000 yards that you have to play.

You may be a little confused by all of that. On its face, it may sound weird that the more lofted clubs (which hit the highest shots) are back in your stance so that you can hit down on the ball more. But the explanation is a simple one. The more the clubface is angled back from vertical, the higher the shot will be. Thus, the only way to get a ball that is lying on the ground up in the air is by exerting downward pressure.

Figure 1-16

When you use a wedge, place the ball in the middle of your stance.

As the club gets longer, the ball moves targetward.

The eyes have it

I see a lot of players setting up to shots with their chins on their chests. Or, if they've been told not to do that, their heads are held so high they can barely see the ball. Neither, of course, is exactly conducive to good play (see Figure 1-17).

Figure 1-17

Don't put your chin on your chest.

But don't lose sight of the ball either!

So how should you be holding your head? The answer is in your eyes. Look down at the ball, which is in what optometrists call your gaze center. Your gaze center is about the size of a Frisbee. Everything outside your gaze center is in your peripheral vision. Now lift your head or drop it slightly. As your head moves, so do your eyes, and so does the ball — into your peripheral vision. Now you can't see the ball so well. Keep your head steady enough to keep the ball inside the Frisbee, and you can't go too far wrong (see Figure 1-18).

Figure 1-18

Keep the ball in the middle of your "gaze center."

That dictates the position of your head.

One hand away

One last thing about your address position. Let your arms hang so that the butt end of the club is one hand away from the inside of your left thigh, as shown in Figure 1-19. You should use this position for every club in the bag except for your putter.

The butt end of the club is a useful guide to check whether the relationship between your hands and the clubhead is correct. With a wedge, for example, the butt end of the club should be in line with the middle of your left thigh. For a driver, it should be opposite your zipper. As before, every other club is between those parameters.

Well, I've talked about a lot of stuff, and I haven't even taken a cut at it yet. Work hard on these preswing routines. After you get yourself in position to move the club away from the ball, forget your address position and concentrate on your swing. It's now time to do what you were sent here to do: create some turbulence. Now I'll get on with the swing.

Figure 1-19

The club should be one hand from your body.

The shaft of a wedge should point at the crease in your left pant leg (or the middle of your thigh).

A driver should point at your zipper.

Starting the Swing: Train Hands/Arms First

Many people think that the most effective way to develop a consistent golf swing is to stand on the range whacking balls until you get it right. But the best way to develop a consistent golf swing is to break the swing down into pieces. Only after you have the first piece mastered should you move on to the next one. I start with what I call miniswings.

Miniswings: Hands and arms

Position yourself in front of the ball as I described earlier in this chapter. Now, without moving anything except your hands, wrists, and forearms, rotate the club back until the shaft is horizontal to the ground and the toe of the club is pointing up. The key to this movement is the left hand, which must stay in the space that it is now occupying, in its address position (see Figure 1-20). The left hand is the fulcrum around which the "swing" rotates. The feeling you should have is one of the butt of the club staying in about the same position while your hands lift the clubhead.

After you get the hang of that little drill, graduate to hitting shots with your miniswing. Let the club travel through 180 degrees, with the shaft parallel to the ground on the backswing and then back to parallel on the through-swing; your follow-through should be a mirror-image of the backswing. The ball obviously doesn't go far with this drill, but your hands and arms are doing exactly what you want them to do through impact on a full swing. Cock the wrists, hit the ball, recock the wrists.

After you have this down, it's time to turn on the horsepower and get your body involved in the action.

Figure 1-20

From address, push down with your left hand as you pull up with your right.

Rotate the club back until the shaft is horizontal, the toe pointing up.

The body

One of the most effective ways for your brain to master something like the golf swing is to set the motion to music. We all learned our ABCs by putting the letters to song. I have played some of my best golf while internally humming a Hootie and the Blowfish single. Music plays a definite role in the learning process.

When you start to move the club and your body into the swing, think of a melody. Make the song real music. Rap, with its staccato rhythm, is no good. To me, that suggests too much independent movement. The golf swing should be a smooth motion, so your song should reflect that smoothness. Think of Tony Bennett, not Coolio.

Anyway, here's the first step toward adding body movement to the hands and arms motion described in the preceding section. Stand as if at address, your arms crossed over your chest so that your right hand is on your left shoulder and your left hand is on your right shoulder. Hold a club horizontally against your chest with both hands, as shown in Figure 1-21.

Figure 1-21

Left hand on right shoulder, right hand on left shoulder, place a club across your chest.

Then turn the club with your shoulders through 90 degrees.

Now turn as if you are making a backswing. Turn so that the shaft turns through 90 degrees, to the point where the shaft is perpendicular to your toe line. As you do so, allow your left knee to move inward so that it points to the golf ball. But the real key is that your right leg must retain the flex that you introduced at address. Retain the flex, and the only way to get the shaft into position is by turning your body. You can't sway or slide to the right and create that 90-degree angle artificially. The turning to the right in your backswing should feel as if you are turning around the inside of your right leg so that your back is facing the target. That's the perfect top-of-the-backswing position.

Unwinding

From the top (note that your spine angle must also remain in the same position from address to the top of the backswing), you must learn the proper sequence so that your body unwinds back to the ball.

The uncoiling starts from the ground and moves up. The first thing to move is your left knee. Your knee must shift toward the target until your kneecap is over the middle of your left foot, where it stops. Any more and your legs start to slide past the ball. A shaft stuck in the ground just outside your left foot is a good check that this move hasn't gone too far. If your knee hits the shaft, stop and try again.

Next, your left hip slides targetward until it is over your knee and foot. Again, the shaft provides a deterrent to your hip going too far.

Pay particular attention to the shaft across your chest in this phase of the swing (work in front of a mirror if you can). The shaft should always parallel the slope of your shoulders as you work your body back to the ball.

Finishing: Looking the part

"Swing" through the impact area all the way to the finish. Keep your left leg straight and let your right knee touch your left knee, as shown in Figure 1-22. Hold this position until the ball hits the ground to prove that you have swung in balance.

If you can do all these things, you're going to look like a real player pretty quickly. Looking the part at least is important. Think about it. Get up on the first tee looking like a schlep who doesn't know how to stand to the ball or make a balanced follow-through, and you're expected to play badly. You don't need excuses. But if you get up to the tee and make the swing I described, passersby are going to stop and watch. And you can have a lot of excuses if you look good. People think you're just unlucky, especially if you look shocked that your shot hit a pedestrian going to the mall three blocks away.

Figure 1-22

Don't slide into the shaft outside your left leg.

Instead, turn your left hip inside the shaft.

Wrong   Right

Putting everything together

Practice each of these exercises for as long as you need to. After you put them together, you have the basis of a pretty good golf swing, one that is a combination of hands/arms and body motion.

- Practice your miniswing.

- Hum a mellow tune.

- Turn your shoulders so that your back is facing the target.

- Put a shaft in the ground — don't slide.

- At finish, keep your left leg straight and your right knee toward left.

Coordinating all these parts into a golf swing takes time. The action of the parts will soon become the whole, and you will develop a feel for your swing. Only repetition from hitting practice balls will allow the student to gain this information. Knowledge, in this case, does not come from reading a book. So get out there and start taking some turf!

Key on the rhythm of your swing. There comes a point in every golfer's life where you just have to "let it go." You can work on your mechanics as much as you want, but the moment to actually hit a ball arrives for all of us. And when that moment comes, you can't be thinking about anything except, perhaps, one simple swing key, or swing thought. That's why top golfers spend most of their time trying to get into what they call "the zone."

The zone is a state of uncluttered thought, where good things happen without any conscious effort from you. You know the kind of thing. The rolled-up ball of paper you throw at the trash can goes in if you just toss the wad without thinking. The car rounds the corner perfectly if you are lost in your thoughts.

In golfing terms, getting into the zone is clearing your mind so that your body can do its job. The mind is a powerful asset, but it can hurt you, too. Negative thoughts about where your ball might go are not going to help you make your best swing. Of course, getting into the zone is easier said than done.

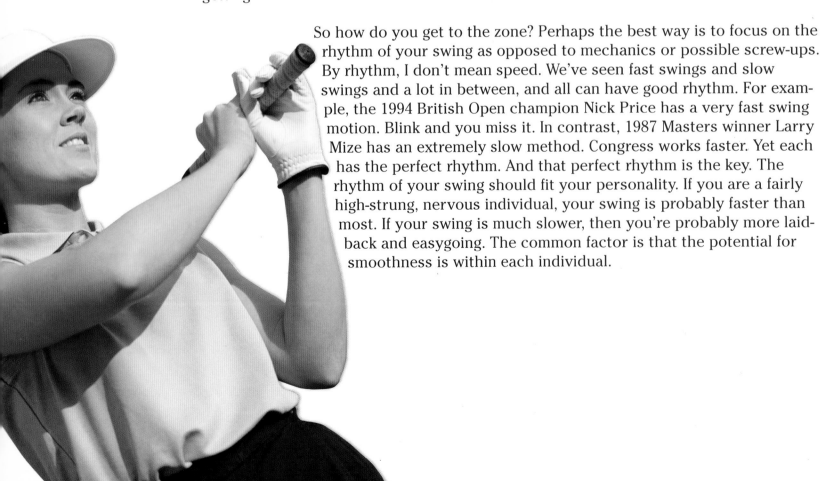

So how do you get to the zone? Perhaps the best way is to focus on the rhythm of your swing as opposed to mechanics or possible screw-ups. By rhythm, I don't mean speed. We've seen fast swings and slow swings and a lot in between, and all can have good rhythm. For example, the 1994 British Open champion Nick Price has a very fast swing motion. Blink and you miss it. In contrast, 1987 Masters winner Larry Mize has an extremely slow method. Congress works faster. Yet each has the perfect rhythm. And that perfect rhythm is the key. The rhythm of your swing should fit your personality. If you are a fairly high-strung, nervous individual, your swing is probably faster than most. If your swing is much slower, then you're probably more laid-back and easygoing. The common factor is that the potential for smoothness is within each individual.

Waggle/swing trigger

Good rhythm during your swing doesn't just happen. Only on those days when you are in the zone will you not have to give your swing encouragement. The rest of the time, you need to set the tone for your swing with your waggle. A waggle is a motion with the wrists in which the hands stay pretty much stationary over the ball and the clubhead moves back a foot or two as if starting the swing (see Figure 1-23). In fact, a waggle is a bit like the mini-swing drill I described in the section "Miniswings: Hands and arms," earlier in this chapter.

Waggling the club serves two main purposes.

> ✔ Waggling is a rehearsal of the crucial opening segment of the backswing.
>
> ✔ If done properly, waggling sets the tone for the pace of the swing. In other words, if you have a short, fast swing, make short, fast waggles. If your swing is of the long and slow variety, make the same kind of waggles. Keep within your species.
>
> ✔ Make that three purposes. In golf, you don't want to start from a static position. You need a "running" start to build up momentum and to prevent your swing from getting off to an abrupt, jerky beginning.
>
> ✔ Waggling the clubhead eases tension you may be feeling and introduces movement into your setup.

Figure 1-23

But the waggle is only the second-to-last thing you do before the backswing begins. The last thing is your swing trigger. Your swing trigger can be any kind of move. For example, 1989 British open champion Mark Calcavecchia shuffles his feet. Gary Player, winner of nine major championships, kicks his right knee in toward the ball. A slight turning of the head to the right is Jack Nicklaus' cue to start his swing. Your swing trigger is up to you. Do whatever frees you up to get the club away from the ball. Create the flow!

After you play golf a while, you can identify players you know from hundreds of yards away by their mannerisms, preshot routine, waggle, and swing trigger. In fact, you can set your watch by good players. Good players take the same amount of time and do exactly the same things before every single shot. And that consistency should be your goal, too. Make yourself recognizable!

When I started working with Kevin Costner on his golf game for the movie *Tin Cup*, one of the first things we talked about was a preshot routine. Teaching Kevin about the preshot routine this early in his education as a golfer got him to do the same thing every time he approached the ball. We had to get him to look like a real touring pro, and every one of them has his own routine.

Kevin picked up the preshot routine real fast. He would get behind the ball about 6 feet and look at the ball and then the target (seeing the target line in his mind's eye). He would then walk up and put his clubface right behind the ball and put his feet on a parallel line to his target line, which is the best way to establish the correct alignment procedure. He would then look at the target once, give the club a little waggle, and then whack, off the ball went. I made him repeat this routine from the first day we started on his swing.

By the time the golf sequences were shot for the movie, Kevin had the look of a well-seasoned touring pro. In fact, as we were walking down the second hole together in the Bob Hope Chrysler Classic, I asked Kevin where he got all those mannerisms of tugging on his shirt, always stretching his glove by pulling on it, and pulling his pants by the right front pocket. He looked at me and said, "I've been watching you for the past three months." I had no idea I was doing all those things in my preshot routine, so you see that your mannerisms become automatic if you do them enough. By the way, my preshot routine looks a lot better when Kevin Costner does it!

Visualizing shots

As you practice your swing and hit more and more shots, patterns — good and bad — emerge. The natural shape of your shots becomes apparent. Few people hit the ball dead-straight; you'll either fade most of your shots (the ball flies from left to right, as shown in Figure 1-24) or draw the majority (the ball moves from right to left in the air). If either tendency gets too severe and develops into a full-blooded slice or hook (a slice is a worse fade, and a hook is a worse draw), stop. Then go for lessons. At this stage, your faults tend to be obvious, certainly to the trained eye. So one session with your local pro should get you back on track.

Figure 1-24

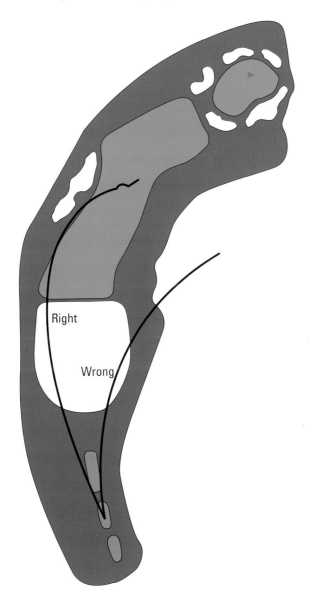

A lesson is important. Faults left to fester and boil soon become ingrained into your method. When that happens, eradicating them becomes a lengthy, expensive process. The old adage comes to mind: "Pay me now, or pay me later." Pay him early so it's easier to fix.

Anyway, after you've developed a consistent shape of shot, you can start to visualize how that shape fits the hole you're on. Then, of course, you know exactly where to aim whether the hole is a dogleg right (turns right), dogleg left (turns left), or straight away. You're a real golfer. Get some plaid pants!

Roll the film — take 83 — action!

When you put together all the connected parts I discuss in this chapter, they should flow into a swing. The first time you see yourself swinging on a picture or a tape, you will swear that that person is not you. What your swing feels like versus what really occurs can be deceiving.

The golf swing is nothing more than a bunch of little motions that are learned, becoming a total motion that is remembered. The tempo and rhythm are applied to the motion through your personality. Those individuals who go fast in life swing fast; those who go slow swing accordingly.

If you can gain the basic mechanics through this book and then apply your own personality, your swing should bloom into something unique. Work hard to understand your swing and watch how other people swing at the ball. The great Ben Hogan told me he would watch other players that he played with. If he liked something they did with their swing, he would go to the practice tee and incorporate that particular move into his swing to see if it worked. What finally came out was a mix of many swings blended to his needs and personality. A champion works very hard.

My golf swing is not the one I used on tour. In 1986, at the age of 38, I started working with Mac O'Grady to revamp my entire swing. Mac gave me a model that I used and blended with my existing swing, shown in the nine photos of Figure 1-25. What came out is a pretty good-looking golf swing, if I do say so myself. Thanks, Mac, for at least making me look good!

Figure 1-25

Address: The calm before the chaos. All systems are go and flight is imminent.

Monitor your swing speed at this time. Checking to see if my seatbelts are fastened.

Turn and stay balanced over your feet. Feel the sun and breeze on your face.

I've reached the top. I'm in attack mode, my swing is growing teeth.

The start down is a slooooooow accumulation of speed. At this time, I've forgotten the sun and wind on my face.

I've organized my chaos. Liftoff is precise. My soul feels the ball.

The hit is relayed up from the shaft to my hands, through my arms into my command center. Post-impact, I feel I've been here forever.

My first glimpse at the sphere that is targetbound. The anxieties of flight and destination consume my brain.

Who cares where it went? I look good enough to be on the top of a golf trophy.

Chapter 2

Developing Your Own Swing

In This Chapter

▸ Defining your golf personality
▸ Checking out your swing plane

*T*his chapter comes with the golfing equivalent of a government health warning. The information on the next few pages isn't for everyone. That's not to say that anything in this chapter is incorrect; it isn't. But for a lot of you — especially if you're at an early stage of your development as a golfer — it will be too much to assimilate. Brain warp. Little puffs of smoke will be coming from your ears.

So you need to know yourself psychologically and how much information you are able to retain. Say you just bought a personal computer with 450 MHz Pentium processor, 128MB RAM, and 14GB on your hard drive. You're sailing with a 3-D accelerator card and a DVD-ROM drive and have 56K modem capabilities. You're ready to rumble. You get home in a flash and start tearing the boxes to pieces. You hook this cable to that port and put this on top of that. You're flying by the seat of your pants and have no idea what you're doing, but you do it anyway. Gone is the idea of looking at the instructions or reading any print data on how to assemble this new computer.

If that scenario sounds like you, skip this chapter. You already know all you need to know about the golf swing — at least for now.

If, however, you are the type who takes a computer home, reads everything in the box, and goes from page 1 to the end of the instruction manual as you piece the computer together, then you're going to want to know more about the golf swing before you can play with confidence. Read on to better understand the complexities of the swing.

What Type of Golfer Are You?

My friend, renowned teacher Peter Kostis, breaks golfers into four types:

- **Analytics** are organized types. You can always spot their desks — the neat ones — in the office.

- **Drivers,** as you'd expect, like to work. They do whatever it takes to get something done.

- **Amiables** are easy to deal with. They accept whatever advice you offer without asking too many questions.

- **Expressives** don't mind any environment they happen to find themselves in; they adjust to whatever comes their way.

In golfing terms, an analytic is someone like Nick Faldo or Bernhard Langer. Jack Nicklaus, Tom Kite, and Tom Watson are drivers. Nancy Lopez, Fred Couples, and Ben Crenshaw are amiables. And Fuzzy Zoeller and Lee Trevino are classic expressives.

Drivers and analytics don't play like amiables and expressives. For a driver or analytic to score well, he needs confidence in his mechanics. An amiable or expressive doesn't. If he feels like he's playing okay, then his swing must be okay, too.

The following situation clarifies these differences. Four of the greatest golfers of our time are playing an exhibition. Lee Trevino, Ben Crenshaw, Jack Nicklaus, and Nick Faldo are scheduled to tee off at Running Rut Golf Course precisely at 11 a.m. Because of a mix-up with the courtesy cars that pick up the players and deliver them to the golf course (Jack and Nick don't like the color of their car; Freddy and Ben could care less), the players are late getting to Running Rut Golf Course.

When the players arrive, with only ten minutes to tee off, the analytic (Faldo) and the driver (Nicklaus) run out to hit balls before playing. Faldo has to swing to gain confidence, and Nicklaus has to hit balls because he likes to work at it.

The other two guys are in the locker room putting on their golf shoes. Trevino is in deep conversation with the locker room attendant about the virtues of not having to tune up his Cadillac for 100,000 miles due to the technologies of the North Star System. Crenshaw is puffing on a cigarette, telling a club member that he was totally flabbergasted yesterday when three 40-foot putts lipped out and just about cost him his sanity. The expressive (Trevino) and the amiable (Crenshaw) don't have to hit balls to get ready. They just go about their business and don't worry about much.

By the way, the match is called off when Faldo and Nicklaus refuse to come to the tee because Nick finds something on the practice tee that he wants to work on and Nicklaus ends up redesigning the practice range. I was told later that the locker room attendant bought Trevino's old Cadillac.

At this stage of your development, being an amiable or an expressive is to your advantage. Because of the enormous amount of new information that you have to absorb, anything that prevents confusion is good.

Having said that, this chapter is for all you analytics and drivers out there. Amiables and expressives, see you in Chapter 3.

Establishing Your Swing Plane

The *swing plane* at its most basic is the path the clubshaft follows when you swing. Unfortunately, other factors affect your swing plane, including your height, weight, posture, flexibility, the thickness of your torso, and the dew point. The plane of your swing can get complicated — especially if you want to cover all the possible variations in the plane from address to the end of the follow-through.

At this point, for all you amiables and expressives, let me expound on the idea of not thinking about the plane of your swing but about the shape of your swing. Two of the best players in the game today — Greg Norman and Bruce Lietzke — have totally different planes to their swings. The golf swing consists of different planes that are shifted during the course of the swing. For example, Greg Norman shifts the plane of his swing initially on the backswing to the outside a little, and then shifts the plane on the downswing to the inside to hit the ball for his particular curve of the ball (*draw*). Bruce shifts the plane of his swing initially on the backswing to the inside and then shifts the plane on the downswing to the outside to hit the ball for his particular curve of the golf ball (*fade*).

So you can see in all this nonsense that there is no one plane in the golf swing. The plane is always shifting in the swing. The swing is an ongoing thing that can get real complicated. Because I'm an expressive, I like to think of the swing not on a plane but in a certain shape. I like to have a picture in my mind of a certain swing shape and forget about the plane of my swing. One picture is geometry, and one is art. I was never good at geometry.

I feel better having said that, so now all you analytics and drivers out there can chew on this plane thing.

The plane of your swing is dictated to a large extent by the clubshaft's angle at address. The swing you make with a wedge in your hands is naturally more upright — or should be — than the swing you make with a driver. The driver has a longer shaft than the wedge and a flatter *lie* (the angle at which the shaft emerges from the clubhead).

For this book, I'm assuming that you maintain the plane you establish at address throughout the swing. For most players, this assumption isn't always the case. If a player's favored shot is one that bends a great deal in the air, the swing plane is tilted either to the right or to the left to compensate for the ball's flight. But if you're trying to hit straight shots, one consistent plane is the way for you.

Mastering the checkpoints

The easiest way to ensure that you maintain your swing is on plane is to have a series of checkpoints, as shown in Figure 2-1. By the way, I'm assuming that you're swinging a driver and that you are right-handed. (To analyze your swing, use a video, a stillframe, or a mirror, or have someone watch you.)

Figure 2-1

Start with the shaft at 45 degrees to the ground.

At the top, the shaft should be parallel with a line along your heels.

Impact should look a lot like address, except that the hips are opening to the target.

✔ The first checkpoint is at address. The shaft starts at a 45-degree angle to the ground.

✔ Now swing the club back until your left arm is horizontal. At that point, the club's butt end (the end of the grip) points directly at the target line. (The target line is the line that exists between the target and the ball. That line also continues forward past the target in a straight line and beyond the ball going in the opposite direction in a straight line. What I'm talking about in this case is one long, straight line.) If the end of the grip is pointing to the target line, you're on plane. If the end of the grip points above the target line, your swing is too flat, or *horizontal*; if the grip end is below the target line, your swing is too upright, or *vertical*.

✔ At the top of your backswing, the club should be parallel with a line drawn along your heels. That's on plane. If the club points to the right of that line, you have crossed the line and will probably hook the shot. A club pointing to the left of that line is said to be *laid off*. In that case, expect a slice.

✔ Halfway down, at the point where your left arm is again horizontal, the shaft's butt end should again point at the target line. This position and the one described in the second bullet in this list are, in effect, identical in swing plane terms.

✔ Impact is the most important point in the golf swing. If the clubface is square when it contacts the ball, what you do anywhere else doesn't really matter. But if you want to be consistent, try to visualize impact as being about the same as your address position, except your hips are aimed more to the left of the target than at the address position, and your weight is shifting to the left side.

Now remember, this method of mastering your checkpoints is a perfect-world situation. Your size, flexibility, and swing shape will probably produce different results. Don't be alarmed if you don't fit this model; not more than a dozen players on the Tour fit this model. Like anything else, there's room for deviation.

At the top

Take a closer look at the top of the backswing. If you can get the club on plane at the top of the backswing, a good shot is more likely.

Look for four things in your backswing:

✔ Your left arm and your shoulders must be on the same slope. In other words, your arm and shoulders are parallel.

✔ The top of your swing is basically controlled by your right arm, which forms a right angle at the top of the swing (see Figure 2-2). Your elbow is about a dollar bill's length away from your rib cage.

Figure 2-2

Your right arm should form a right angle at the elbow.

✔ Your shoulders turn so that they are at 90 degrees to the target line.

✔ The clubface is angled parallel to your left arm and your shoulders. Your left wrist controls this position. Ideally, your wrist angle remains unchanged from address to the top. That way, the relationship between the clubface and your left arm is constant. If your wrist angle does change, the clubface and your left arm are going to be on different planes — and that's a problem.

If your wrist does change, it is either bowed or cupped (see Figure 2-3). A *bowed* (bent forward) left wrist at the top causes the clubface to look skyward in what is called a *closed* position. From that position, a hook is likely. A *cupped* (bent back) wrist means that the clubface is more visible to someone looking you in the face. A cupped wrist leads to an open position, which probably results in a slice.

Of course, playing good golf from an open or closed position at the top of the backswing is possible but more difficult. To do well, your swing has to have some kind of built-in compensation, which is the only way you can square the clubface at impact. And compensations take a lot of practice. Only if you have the time to hit hundreds of balls a week can you ever hope to improve from an inherently flawed swing. Even then, that compensated swing is going to be tough to reproduce under pressure. For examples, watch Corey Pavin (open) and Lee Trevino (closed).

Anyway, swing sequences tend to show three very different methods. The legendary Sam Snead crosses the line at the top and comes over every shot to get the ball to go straight. Solheim Cup player Annika Sorenstam is the opposite. She lays the club off at the top. And 1995 PGA champion Steve Elkington is on plane. Make his swing your model, and you can't go too far wrong.

Figure 2-3

When your left wrist is "bowed," watch out for a hook.

When your left wrist is "cupped," watch out for a slice.

Going Where Others Have Gone Before

No matter what your playing level, a great way to improve is to watch other players, particularly those with some of the same characteristics that you have. Watch for similarities in body size, pace, and shape of swing — even the kinds of mistakes they make under pressure.

One way to start is to identify your goals. Do you want to emulate the master of the long game, John Daly, who regularly blasts drives beyond 300 yards? Or do you want to concentrate on following some experts in the short game, such as Seve Ballesteros, Walter Hagen, and Patty Sheehan? Phil Mickelson has a great lob wedge and sand wedge. Phil Rodgers, with his unique chipping techniques, is a short-game guru.

If you want to follow some really fine putting, keep your eyes peeled for Isao Aoki of Japan, who displays a unique putting stroke acutely tailored to Japanese grass. Former PGA champion Jacki Burke was one of the greatest short putters of all time. Some of the best putters in the world today are Ben Crenshaw and Phil Mickelson, with their long, slow putts, as well as Jim Furych, David Duval, and Mark O'Meara. Nancy Lopez was another great putter in her heyday.

Maybe you want to work on something much more specific. In terms of different swing shapes, every golfer has something to illustrate. Keep a close eye on the golfers who swing like you do, and you may notice something about them that makes their drives sail those 300 yards down the fairway.

Look at those people who have short swings (the club doesn't get to parallel at the top of their swings): Amy Alcott, Lee Trevino, and John Cook. Long-flowing swings you can find here: John Daly, Vicki Goetze, and Phil Mickelson. If you want to look at people who change the shapes of their swings in mid-swing, look at Bruce Lietzke and Jim Furyk, but not for too long — you might go blind!

Some players, like Nancy Lopez, cross the line at the tops of their swings (the club points to the right of the target). Other players, like Ernie Els, have the club laid-off at the top of the swing (pointing to the left of the target at the top of the swing). If you like rhythm and balance, watch Patty Sheehan, and check out pictures of Sam Snead's swing.

Maybe swing speed is your demon. Are you trying too hard to copy someone you admire, or are you making sure that the pace you use is as natural for you as Tour golfers' swings are for them? Ben Crenshaw, Nancy Lopez, Scott Simpson, and Jay Haas have slow-paced swings.

Larry Mize's swing is extremely slow. Steve Elkington, Davis Love III, Jack Nicklaus, Sam Snead, Annika Sorenstam, and Lee Janzen have medium-paced swings. Fast swings belong to Ben Hogan, Lanny Wadkins, Tom Watson, and Dan Pohl. Nick Price's is very fast. And all these players are very good.

Hand size can affect grip; grip can affect your swing. Watch how these players use their hands. Billy Casper and Dave Stockton use their wrists to create momentum in the club-head with their putting strokes. Canadian Dave Barr uses the ten-finger grip. Fred Couples uses the cross-handed grip for putting. Jack Nicklaus uses the interlocking grip for his golf swing. Tom Kite uses the interlocking grip for full swings and the cross-handed grip for putting.

Maybe you want to keep tabs on golfers who have modified their games to see how a pro adapts his or her game, either to combat the yips, as did Bernhard Langer, who invented his own grip, and Sam Snead, who putted sidesaddle, or to accommodate a new tool, like Bruce Lietzke's and Orville Moody's long, long putters.

Or maybe your goals are larger than that — you don't care about all these little tricks and habits; you just want to win. Or you're only looking for a few hours of fresh air and fun. Notice how the attitudes of famous players affect not only how they play but also how much they enjoy the game. Nancy Lopez's amiability and ability to keep her cool make her one of the most popular personalities on the LPGA Tour. Fred Couples and Ben Crenshaw are also amiable golfers. Mark O'Meara is one of the rare pro golfers who truly enjoys Pro-Am tournaments.

Seve Ballesteros is a gutsy player who plays with great imagination and creativity. Arnold Palmer is a master of special shots and also a bold golfer. Other daring players include John Daly and Laura Davies, who are as fun and exciting to watch as expressive golfers Lee Trevino and Fuzzy Zoeller. Meg Mallon is always trying something new and winds up having great fun with the game.

On the other end of the attitude spectrum, you'll find Jackie Burke, who created intense drills for himself so that he knew all about pressure: His motivation was to win. Lee Janzen is a fierce competitor, not unlike Ben Hogan, who was himself a steely competitor and a perfectionist, and who surrendered finally not to any other player but to the yips. (See Chapter 3 for more on the yips.) Betsy King's tenacity earned her 20 tournaments in the span of five years. Greg Norman plays to win and is willing to take risks to do it. Other hard-working perfectionists include Tom Kite, Jack Nicklaus, Tom Watson, and Annika Sorenstam.

A conservative style of play is the trademark of Tom Kite and of Mike Reid. Nick Faldo is an analytic golfer.

Finally, there are some players you just can't go wrong watching — they've done so well that they must be doing some things right!

- Bobby Jones was the winner of the 1930 Grand Slams.

- Gary Player is the winner of nine major championships, including all four majors.

- Steve Elkington was the 1995 PGA champion.

- Tommy Armour won a U.S. Open, a British Open, and a PGA championship.

- Lee Trevino won the U.S. Open, the British Open, and the PGA championship twice and has become one of the top players on the Senior Tour.

- Bernhard Langer and Larry Mize have both won the Masters.

- Mark Calcavecchia and Nick Price were British Open champions. Price was the best golfer in the field from 1992 to 1994.

- Walter Hagen was a five-time PGA champion, winner of the British Open four times and the U.S. Open twice.

- Harry Vardon holds the record for the most British Open wins — six in all.

- Sam Snead won 81 tournaments on the PGA Tour.

- Annika Sorenstam won the Women's Open in 1995 and 1996. She also played the Solheim Cup.

- Laura Davies won 17 times through 1998.

- Babe Zaharias, an award-winning athlete, won 31 events and ten major titles in her eight years on the LPGA Tour.

- Nancy Lopez has won 48 times on the LPGA Tour.

- Mickey Wright has won 82 times during her LPGA career.

- Kathy Whitworth has won more times than anybody: 88 times, including six major championships. She was named player of the year seven times.

- Hall of Famer Betsy King won 20 tournaments between 1984 and 1989.

- Hall of Famer JoAnne Carner has won 42 events.

- Hall of Famer Pat Bradley was the first LPGA player to pass the $4 million milestone.

Chapter 3

Putting: The Art of Rolling the Ball

In This Chapter

▸ Putting styles

▸ Visualizing the hole

▸ Mastering the basics

▸ Short putts versus long putts

▸ Dealing with the yips

This chapter is an important part of this book. Statistically, putting is 68 percent of the game of golf, so you may want to take notes. You can't score well if you can't putt — it's that simple. If you want proof, look at the top professionals on tour who average about 29 putts per round. In other words, these professionals are one-putting at least 7 of the 18 greens in a round of golf. The average score on tour isn't 7 under par, so even these folks are missing their fair share of greens. And where are they retrieving their mistakes? That's right: with their short game and putting.

Because most women can't physically drive the ball hundreds of yards, they can focus on refining their short game skills, such as chipping, pitching, and putting. Remember, a solid putt counts the same on the scorecard as a 200-yard drive.

No other part of golf induces as much heartache and conversation as putting. Many fine strikers of the ball have literally been driven from the sport because they couldn't finish holes as well as they started them. Why? Because putting messes with your internal organs. Every putt has only two possibilities: You either miss it or hole it. Accept that and you won't have nightmares about the ones that "should" have gone in.

You Gotta Be You

Putting is the most individual part of this individual game. You can putt — and putt successfully — in a myriad of ways. You can break all the rules with a putter in your hands as long as the ball goes in the hole. Believe me, you can get the job done by using any number of methods. You can make long, flowing strokes like Phil Mickelson, Ben Crenshaw, and Vicki Goetze. Or shorter, firmer, "pop" strokes like Corey Pavin and Gary Player. Or you can create the necessary momentum in the clubhead with your wrists — Dave Stockton and Billy Casper are living proof of how well that can work. Or if none of these styles appeals to you, you can go to a long, "witch's broom-handle" putter. Both Orville Moody and Bruce Lietzke did and have enjoyed a lot of success. Putt variety has to do with stroke length. Even on the longest putts, the "swing" required is still less than that for a short chip shot from just off the green.

Putting is more about those ghostly intangibles — feel, touch, and nerve — than about mechanics. My feeling is that getting too involved with putting mechanics is a mistake. You can have the most technically perfect stroke in the world and still be like an orangutan putting a football on the greens — if you don't have the touch, that is. Even more than the rhythm and tempo of your full swing, your putting stroke and demeanor on the greens should reflect your own personality. Your hands probably shouldn't be "behind" the ball at impact, but other than that, your style is up to you.

Be aware that if any aspect of this often-infuriating game was ever designed to drive you to distraction, it's putting. Putting may look simple — and sometimes it is — but some days you just know there's no way that little ball at your feet is going to make its way into that hole. You know it, your playing partners know it, your financial consultant knows it, everyone knows it. Putting is mystical; it comes and goes like the tide.

It's All in Your Head

In putting, visualization is everything. You can visualize in two ways: Either you see the hole as very small, or so big that any fool can drop the ball in. The former, of course, is infinitely more damaging to your psyche than the latter. When you imagine that the hole shrinks, the ball doesn't seem to fit. You can tell yourself that the ball is 1.68 inches in diameter and the hole 4.25 inches across all you want, but the fact remains that the ball is too big. I know; I've been there. It won't fit. It just won't fit no matter what I do. About this time, I usually seek psychiatric care and surround myself with pastel colors.

And on other days, happily, the hole is so big that putting is like stroking a marble into a wine barrel. Simply hit the ball, and boom, it goes in. When this happens to you, savor every moment. Drink in the feeling and bathe in it so that you don't forget it — because you may not take another bath for a long time.

The crazy thing is that these two scenarios can occur on consecutive days, sometimes even in consecutive rounds. I've even experienced both feelings on consecutive holes. Why? I've no idea. Figuring out why is way beyond my feeble intellect. Try not to think too deeply about putting.

Building Your Stroke

As I've already said, you can achieve good putting by using any number of methods or clubs. But I'm going to ignore that when talking about putting basics. At this stage, you should putt in as orthodox a manner as possible. That way, when something goes wrong — which it will — the fault is easier to fix because you know where to look. That's the trouble with unorthodoxy. It's hard to find order in chaos.

The putting grip

The putting grip isn't like the full-swing grip. The full-swing grip is more in the fingers, which encourages the hinging and unhinging of your wrists. Your putting grip's goal is to achieve exactly the opposite effect. You grip the putter more in the palm of your hands to reduce the amount of movement your hands must make. Although you may putt well despite a lot of wrist action in your stroke, I prefer that you take the wrists out of play as much as possible. Unless you have incredible touch, your wrists are not very reliable when you need to hit the ball short distances consistently. You're far better off relying on the rocking of your shoulders to create momentum in the putterhead.

Not all putting grips are the same — not even those grips where you place your right hand below the left in conventional fashion. But what all putting grips do have in common is that the palms of both hands face each other, so your hands can work together in the stroke. The last thing you want is your hands fighting one another. Too much right hand, and your ball has a bad experience. If your left hand dominates, your right hand sues for nonsupport. Both hands need to work together for a good experience and no legal hassles.

Your hands can join together in one of two ways, shown in Figure 3-1. (I describe a more advanced method of gripping the club in the following section, "Left hand low.") Go with the grip that you find most comfortable.

- Place the palms of your hands on either side of the club's grip. Slide your right hand down a little so that you can place both hands on the club. You should feel like you are going to adopt the ten-finger grip (see Chapter 1).

- Place your left index finger over the little finger of your right hand. Known as the "reverse overlap," this is probably the most-used putting grip on the PGA and LPGA Tours.

- Extend your left index finger down the outside of the fingers of your right hand until the tip touches your right index finger. I call this grip the "extended reverse overlap." The left index finger, when extended, provides stability to the putting stroke.

Figure 3-1

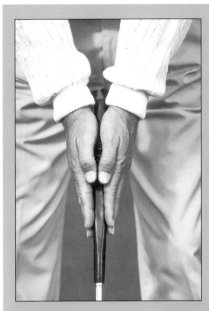

Place your palms on opposing sides of the grip.

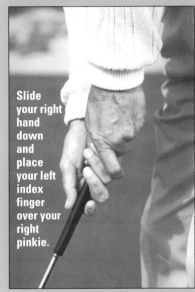

Slide your right hand down and place your left index finger over your right pinkie.

Or extend your left index finger over the fingers of your right hand.

Left hand low

This method is commonly referred to as *cross-handed*. The left hand hangs below the right with the putter (or vice versa if you're a lefty). This method is used by many players today because it helps keep the lead hand (the left, in this case) from bending at the wrist as you hit the ball. (See Figure 3-2.)

One of the biggest causes of missed putts is the breaking down of the left wrist through impact. The left wrist bends through impact, causing the putter blade to twist. This twisting causes the ball to wobble off-line. The bend that your left wrist has at the address position should be maintained throughout the stroke.

The cross-handed grip is said to make maintaining your wrist position easier. Many great players such as Fred Couples and Tom Kite have gone to this type of grip.

The few times I have tried the cross-handed grip, pulling with the left wrist seemed to be easier. It seems that pulling with the lead hand makes it harder to break down with the wrist.

Figure 3-2

A left-hand-below-right putting grip helps stop left-wrist breakdown.

Another reason you see many of today's pros using a cross-handed grip is that with the left arm lower on the shaft, you pull the left shoulder more square to your target line. Pulling your left shoulder happens automatically with this grip. I tend to open my shoulders (aim to the left) with my putter. As soon as I use this type of grip, my left shoulder moves toward the target line, and I'm more square to my line.

I think the best asset that this stroke has to offer is that you swing the left arm back and forth during the stroke. The trailing hand (right) is along for the ride, which is a very good way to stroke your golf ball. I suggest that you try this grip.

Long putters

The difference with using long putters is that the length of the club dictates where you place your hands on the club. The long putter is the final refuge for the neurologically impaired. If you watch any Senior PGA Tour event on television, you see more than a few long putters.

Long putters differ greatly and range from 46 to 52 inches in length. Long putters remove all wrist movement from your putting stroke because your left hand anchors the club to your chest. Your left hand holds the club at the end of the shaft, and your fingers wrap around the grip so that the back of your hand faces the ball. That grip is the fulcrum around which the club swings. Your right hand is basically along for the ride. In fact, your right hand should barely touch the club. Your right hand's only role is to pull the club back and follow the club through.

Long putters are easy on the nerves, which is why these clubs enjoy such popularity on the Senior Tour. Although, to be fair, Senior Tour players are not alone. No fewer than three members of the European Ryder Cup team in 1995 used long putters. And all three members won their singles matches on the final afternoon, perhaps the most pressure-filled day in all of golf. So long putters definitely have something. You've got nothing to lose by trying one.

My first introduction into the advantages of the long putter came, as a lot of my golf knowledge did, from Mac O'Grady. We were playing a practice round at Riveria Country Club for the L.A. Open. Mac was not putting with much distinction at this point and decided to have two neurosurgeons from UCLA's neurological department follow us as we golfed. Mac was writing and financing a study about the yips (discussed later in this chapter) for publication, and these two doctors were helping with the study. The doctors had no background in golf and followed us for nine holes while Mac putted with a 52-inch-long putter and I used my regular 35-inch putter. The doctors had no idea that few golfers use a long putter.

Mac asked the doctors to take notes as we went about our business, and then we got together after the round and discussed the merits of both putting techniques. We first asked the doctors to explain the workings of my stroke with the short putter. One doctor said, "Gary uses bimanual manipulation of the implement that requires a left-right brain synergy because both hands and shoulder movement are constantly monitored by the brain as they are acting together." I ordered a beer.

I swallowed hard and then asked what they thought of Mac's stroke with the long putter. "Mac has isolated the left shoulder and has a fixed fulcrum with the left hand. The right shoulder joint is doing the swinging without the deployment of the right wrist. You have effectively isolated only one side of the brain (the left hemisphere controls the right side and vice versa) because there is no conspiracy going on with only one side controlling the movement. You can deter focal dystonia much longer with this movement." I ordered a Jack Daniels.

The doctors asked the last question of the day: "Why would anyone use that little short putter that Gary uses? It is obviously inferior, as he has to put two hands on it to control the movement. The long putter and its technique are superior for gradient ramp movement." I ordered two aspirins.

Putting posture

After you establish where your eyes should be as you crouch over the ball to putt, you need to be in the correct posture position. You should have a slight knee flex in your putting stance. If your knees are locked in a straight position, you're straining your back too much. Don't bend your knees too much, though, because you may start to look like a golf geek!

You should bend over from your waist so that your arms hang straight down. This stance allows the arms to swing in a pendulum motion, back and forth from a fixed point. Hold your arms straight out from your body as you are standing straight and tall. Now bend down with those arms outstretched from the waist until your arms are pointing to the ground. Then flex your knees a little bit, and you're in the correct putting posture.

Putting: Stand and deliver

You can break a lot of rules in how you stand to hit a putt. (See Figure 3-3.) Ben Crenshaw stands open to the target line, his left foot drawn back. Gary Player does the opposite: He sets up closed, his right foot farther from the target line than his left. But that's their style; I keep things simple with a square stance so that I don't need to make many in-stroke adjustments to compensate for an unorthodox stance.

Figure 3-3

To putt, you can stand open.

Or closed.

Or square.

Toeing the line

As in a full swing, your toe stance line is the key. Regardless of which stance you choose, your toe stance line should always be parallel to your target line (refer to Figure 3-3). Be aware that the target line isn't always a straight line from the ball to the hole — if only putting were that simple. Unfortunately, greens are rarely flat, so putts break or bend either from right to left or from left to right. (See "Reading the break," later in this chapter.) So sometimes you're going to be aiming, say, 5 inches to the right of the hole, and other times maybe a foot to the left. (See Figure 3-4.) Whatever you decide, your toe stance line must always be parallel your target line.

Being parallel to your target line is important. In effect, you make every putt straight. Applying a curve to your putts is way too complicated and affects your stroke. Imagine how you have to adjust if you aim at the hole and then try to push the ball out to the right because of a slope on the green. You have no way to be consistent. Keep putting simple. Remember, on curved putts, aim your feet parallel to the line you have chosen, not to the hole (see Figure 3-5).

Figure 3-4

Sometimes your target isn't the hole.

Sometimes you have to allow for the ball to bend on a sloping green.

Figure 3-5

Standing just right

Okay, now what about width of stance? Again, you have margin for error, but your heels need to be about shoulder-width apart at address, as shown in Figure 3-6.

For putting, your heels should be shoulder-width apart.

You have to bend over to put the putter behind the ball. How far should you bend? Far enough so that your eye line (a much-neglected part of putting) is directly above the ball. To find out how that position feels, place a ball on your forehead between your eyes, bend over, and let the ball drop, as shown in Figure 3-7. Where the ball hits the ground is where the ball should be in relation to your body. The ball shouldn't be to the inside, the outside, behind, or in front of that point. The ball should be right there, dead center. This alignment places your eyes not just over the ball but also over the line that you want the ball to travel.

Drop the ball from a point between your eyes.

Where the ball lands is where it should be positioned in your stance.

Let the shape of your stroke dictate which putter you use

Okay, you've got an idea of how to hold onto your putter and how to stand to hit a putt. The next step is deciding what putter to use. Although you have a lot of putters to choose from, you can eliminate many by knowing the type of putter you are. In other words, the shape of your stroke is the determining factor in the type of putter that you use. Figure 3-8 shows two types of putters.

My good friend and noted teaching professional Peter Kostis explains: Most putting strokes fall into one of two groups, at least in terms of their shapes. They either move "straight back and straight through" with the blade staying square, or "inside to inside," the blade doing a mini-version of the rotation found in a full swing. Conveniently, most putters are suited to a specific stroke shape. There are two main types: face-balanced, center-shafted putters and those that are not face-balanced, such as heel-shafted blades.

Figure 3-8

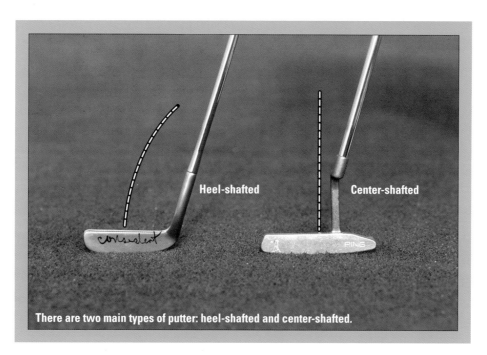

Heel-shafted   Center-shafted

There are two main types of putter: heel-shafted and center-shafted.

The key to success is to match your putter to your stroke. If keeping the blade square in your stroke is important to you, get a face-balanced, center-shafted model. You can test to see whether a putter is face-balanced by resting the shaft on your finger. If the putterface stays parallel to the ground, it is face-balanced.

The inside-to-inside stroke is easier to make on a consistent basis with a heel-shafted putter. It will hang toe-down while resting on your finger.

Be warned, though. Some putters hang at an angle of 45 degrees. They are equally good — or bad! — for either stroke.

Getting up to speed

In the two decades-plus that I played on the PGA Tour, I saw a lot of putters and a lot of different putting methods. The good putters came in all shapes and sizes, too. Some good putters putted in what could be termed mysterious ways, and other good putters were very conventional. So analyzing different putting methods is no help. The best way to look at putting is to break it down to its simplest level. The hole. The ball. The ball fits into the hole. Now get the ball into the hole in the fewest possible strokes.

You have to hit each putt so that the ball rolls at the right speed. If you don't have the speed, you don't know where to aim. The right speed means hitting a putt so that the ball that misses the cup finishes 14 to 18 inches past the hole, as shown in Figure 3-9. This distance is true no matter the length of the putt. Two feet or 40 feet, your aim must be to hit the ball at a pace that will see it finish 14 to 18 inches beyond the hole.

Figure 3-9

Aim to hit every putt so that if it misses, it rolls 14 to 18 inches past the hole.

You're probably wondering why your ball needs the right speed. Well, the right speed gives the ball the greatest chance of going into the hole. Think about it: If the ball rolls toward the middle of the cup, it won't be going so hard that it rolls right over the hole. If the ball touches either side of the cup, it may drop in. The plan is to give the ball every chance to drop in, from any angle — front, back, or side. I don't know about you, but I want that hole to seem as big as possible.

The only putts I know that certainly don't drop are those putts left short of the hole. If you've played golf for any length of time, you've heard the phrase "never up, never in" when you've left a putt 6 inches short of the cup. The phrase is annoying but true. As the Irish say, "99 percent of all putts that come up short don't go in, and the other 1 percent never get there." Remember that saying. Also remember that you should try to make every putt that lands 10 feet from the hole and closer. I hope to make every putt from 10 to 20 feet, and I try to get every putt close from 20 feet and beyond.

Reading the break

After you have the distance control that a consistent pace brings, you can work on the second half of the putting equation: reading the break. The break is the amount a putt moves from right to left or left to right on a green. Slope, topographical features such as water and mountains, the grain of the grass, and, perhaps most important, how hard you hit the ball dictate the break. For example, if I am an aggressive player who routinely hits putts 5 feet past the cup, I'm not going to play as much break as you. (You, remember, hit your putts only 14 to 18 inches past the cup.)

The firmer you hit a putt, the less the ball bends or breaks on even the steepest gradient. So don't be fooled into thinking that there's only one way a putt can be holed. On, say, a 20 footer, you probably have about five possibilities. How hard you hit the ball is one factor.

The key, of course, is consistency, the genesis of putting. Being a bold putter is not a bad thing (if you're willing to put up with the occasional return 5-footer) — as long as you putt that way all the time and are still in your teens.

Anyway, the first thing I do when I arrive at a golf course is to find the natural slope of the terrain. If mountains are in the area, finding the natural slope is easy. Say the mountains are off to your right on the first hole. Any slope is going to be from right to left on that hole. In fact, the slope on every green is going to be "from" the mountain (unless, of course, a particularly humorless architect has decided to bank some holes toward the mountain). So I take that into account on every putt I hit.

If the course is relatively flat, go to the pro or course superintendent. Ask about nearby reservoirs or, failing that, the area's lowest point. This point can be 5 miles away or 20 — it doesn't matter. Find out where that point is and take advantage of gravity. Gravity is a wonderful concept. Every putt breaks down a hill — high point to low point — unless you're in a zero-gravity environment. But that's another book.

After you know the lowest point, look at each green in detail. If you're on an older course, the greens probably slope from back to front because of drainage. Greens nowadays have more humps and undulations than ever and are surrounded by more bunkers. And the sand is the key. The drainage should be designed so that water runs past a bunker and not into the sand. Take that insight into account when you line up a putt. And don't forget the barometric pressure and dew point — just kidding!

Going against the grain

Golf is played on different grasses (hopefully not on the same course), and climate usually determines the kind of grass on a course. Grasses in hot, tropical areas have to be more resilient, so they typically have thick blades. *Bermuda grass* is the most common. Its blades tend to follow the sun from morning to afternoon — in other words, from east to west. Because the blade is so strong, Bermuda grass can carry a golf ball according to the direction in which it is lying. Putts "downgrain" are faster than putts "into" the grain. All that, of course, has an effect on where you have to aim a putt.

Look at the cup to find out which way the grass is growing. Especially in the afternoon, you see a ragged half and a smooth, or sharp, half — the direction in which the grass is growing. The ragged look is caused by the grass's tendency to grow and fray. If you can't tell either way, go to the fringe (the edge of the green). The grass on the fringe is longer, so you can usually see the direction of the grain right away.

Another common type of grass is bent grass. You see bent grass primarily in the northern and northeastern United States. *Bent grass* has a thinner blade than Bermuda grass, but it doesn't stand up to excessive heat as well.

Bent grass is used by many golf course builders because you can get the greens moving real fast, and the recent trend for greens is to combine slope with speed. Try getting on the roof of your car, putting a ball down to the hood ornament, and making it stop. That's the speed of most of the greens on tour with bent grass.

I don't concern myself much with grain on bent greens. I just worry about the slope and the 47 things on my checklist before I putt. Putting could be so much fun if I didn't have a brain.

If you get the chance to play golf in Japan, you'll play on grass called korai. This wiry grass can be a menace on the greens because it's stronger than Astroturf and can really affect the way the ball rolls on the green. If the blades of grass are growing toward you, you have to hit the ball with a violent pop.

Isao Aoki, a great Japanese player, uses a unique putting stroke in which he has the toe of the putter way off the ground and then gives the ball a pop with his wrist to get it going — an effective way of dealing with the korai grass he grew up on.

When dealing with grasses, an architect tries to use the thinnest possible blade, given the climate, and then tries to get that grass to grow straight up to eliminate grain. Bent is better than Bermuda when it comes to growing straight, so grain is rarely a factor on bent greens.

Bobbing for plumbs

Plumb-bobbing is all about determining where vertical is. It lets you determine how much break is present. Plumb-bobbing is one reason — along with polyester pants and plaid jackets — that nongolfers laugh at serious golfers. When a plumb-bobbing golfer pops up on TV, all the nongolfer sees is a guy, one eye closed, standing with a club dangling in front of his face. Actually, if you think about this scenario, the whole thing does look more than a little goofy. I can't honestly say that I am a devotee of the method, although plumb-bobbing works for some people. I use plumb-bobbing only when I'm totally bored on the green or if I think that one of the condos on the course was built on a slant. But if Ben Crenshaw thinks that plumb-bobbing helps, who am I to argue?

The first step in plumb-bobbing is to find your dominant eye. You close the other eye when plumb-bobbing. Here's how to find yours.

Figure 3-10

Make a circle with the thumb and index finger of your right hand a couple of inches in front of your face, as shown in Figure 3-10. Look through the circle at a distant object. Keep both eyes open at this stage. Now close your right eye. Where is the object now? If the object is still in the circle, your left eye is dominant. If, of course, you can still see the object in the circle with your left eye closed, then your right eye is dominant.

Okay, now you're ready to plumb-bob. Put some dancing shoes on and stand as close to the ball as possible. First, keeping your dominant eye open, hold your putter up in front of your face and perpendicular to the ground so that the shaft runs through the ball. Now look to see where the hole is in relation to the shaft. If the hole appears to the right of the club, the ball will break from the shaft to the hole — from left to right. If the hole is on the left, the opposite will be true. (See Figure 3-11.) What plumb-bobbing basically shows is the general slope of the green from your ball to the hole.

Remember that this is about as exact as weather forecasting, but it gives you the vicinity.

Plumb-bobbing is not an exact science. But plumb-bobbing is very cool. People who see you plumb-bobbing will think that you know something they don't. So, if nothing else, fake plumb-bobbing. People will be impressed.

Figure 3-11

Dominant eye open, hold the shaft up perpendicular to the ground and in front of your face.

Where the hole is in relation to the shaft indicates how much a putt will bend.

Short Putts

One of the greatest short putters of all time is former PGA champion Jackie Burke, who today helps Tour player Steve Elkington with his game. I was talking to Jackie one day about putting and asked him how he developed his ability to make short putts. His reply made short putts seem astonishingly simple. All Jackie did was analyze his game to identify his strengths and weaknesses. He concluded that his short game — his pitching and chipping — was where he could pick up strokes on his competitors. Jackie knew that to score really well, he had to be able to make a lot of putts in the 3- to 4-foot range. He felt that most of his chips and pitches would finish 3 to 4 feet from the cup.

So every day, Jackie went to the practice putting green with 100 balls. He stuck his putterhead in the cup, and where the butt end of the club hit the ground, he put a ball. Then he went over to the caddie shed and grabbed a caddie. Jackie handed the guy a $100 bill and told him to sit down behind the cup. If Jackie made all 100 putts, Jackie kept the money. If he missed even one, the caddie pocketed the cash.

Jackie did this routine every day. All of a sudden, every short putt he hit meant something. All short putts counted. And when he got to the golf course and was faced with a short putt, he knew that he had already made 100 of them under a lot of pressure. (A hundred dollar bill in those days was backed by real gold.)

The word *pressure* is the key. You have to create a situation in which missing hurts you. Missing doesn't have to hurt you financially. Any kind of suffering is fine. You have to care about the result of every putt. If all you have to do after missing is pull another ball over and try again, you're never going to get better. You don't care enough.

So put yourself under pressure, even if you only make yourself stay on the green until you can make 25 putts in a row. You'll be amazed at how difficult the last putt is after you've made 24 in a row. The last putt is the same putt in physical terms. But mentally, you're feeling nervous, knowing that missing means that you've wasted your time over the previous 24 shots. In other words, you'll have created tournament conditions on the practice green. Now that's pressure; suck some air.

Because you don't want the ball to travel far, the stroke has to be equally short, which doesn't give the putterhead much of an arc to swing on. But the lack of arc is okay. On a short putt, you don't want the putterhead to move inside or outside the target line (on the way back). So think straight back and straight through. If you can keep the putterface looking directly at the hole throughout the stroke and you are set up squarely, you're going to make more short putts than you miss.

My instructions sound easy, but as with everything else in golf, knowing how short putting feels helps. Lay a 2 x 4 piece of wood on the ground. Place the toe of your putter against the board. Hit some putts, keeping the toe against the board until after impact, as shown in Figure 3-12. Always keep the putterhead at 90 degrees to the board so that the putter moves on the straight-back-and-straight-through path that you want. Practice this drill until you can repeat the sensation on real putts. And remember one of my *Golf For Dummies* secrets: Never allow the wrist on your lead hand to bend when putting. If you do, you'll end up in putting hell.

Figure 3-12

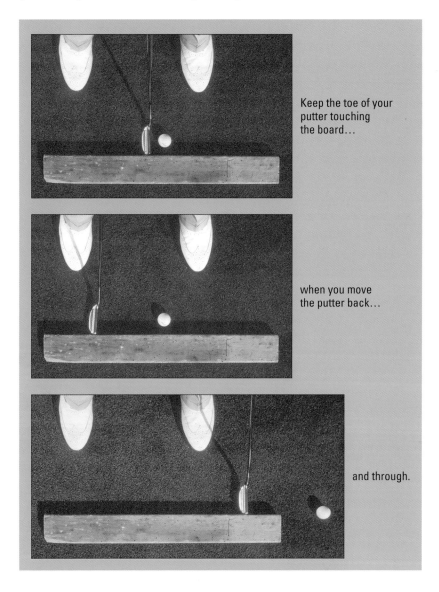

Keep the toe of your putter touching the board...

when you move the putter back...

and through.

Long Putts

If short putts are a test of precision and technique, long putts are a test of your feel for pace. Nothing more. The last thing I want you thinking about over, say, a 40-foot putt is how far back you want to take the putter or what path the putter will follow. Instead, focus on smoothness, rhythm, and timing — all the things that foster control over the distance a ball travels. Or, as Chevy Chase said in the cult golf movie *Caddyshack*, "Be the ball."

The following is how I practice my long putting. First, I don't aim for a hole. I'm thinking distance, not direction. I figure that hitting a putt 10 feet short is a lot more likely than hitting it 10 feet wide, so distance is the key. I throw a bunch of balls down on the practice green and putt to the far fringe (see Figure 3-13). I want to see how close I can get to the edge without going over. I don't care about where I hit the putt, just how far. After a while, you'll be amazed at how adept you become, to the point where, after impact, you can predict with accuracy how far the ball will roll.

Figure 3-13

To get a feel for distance, putt a few balls to the far side of the practice putting green.

One of the basic rules for a beginning golfer is to match the length of your golf swing to your putting stroke. That is, if you have a short golf swing (your left arm, if you're right-handed, doesn't get too far up in the air on your backswing), you should make sure that your putting stroke is a short one. If your golf swing is long, make sure that your putting stroke is long also. Don't fight the forces of contradiction.

Look at two of the greatest putters in the world today, Ben Crenshaw and Phil Mickelson. Both players have long and slow swings, and their putting strokes are the same. On the other hand, you have Nick Price and Lanny Wadkins, who have quick swings and quick putting strokes. They all keep a balance between golf swing and putting stroke.

Your swing tells a lot about your personality. If your golf swing is long and slow, usually you are a very easygoing individual. If your swing is short and fast, you're usually the kind of person who walks around with his hair on fire. So don't mix the two types of swings because that can lead to a contrast in styles within your game.

Making a contradiction in the two, I believe, leads to problems. Sam Snead had a great long putting stroke that went with his beautiful swing, but as the years came on the golf course, the swing stayed long and the stroke got much shorter. The yips took over (see "The Yips," later in this chapter). Johnny Miller had a big swing with his golf clubs and a putting stroke that was so fast you could hardly see it. There was a contradiction, and he had to go to the TV tower because he couldn't roll 'em in anymore. The change wasn't all bad; Johnny adds great insight to the game from his position in the announcing booth.

So keep your two swings — the golf swing and the putting stroke — the same. Keep your mind quiet and create no contradictions between the two swings.

I call my routine "being the ball." Another exercise to foster your feel for distance is what I call the "ladder" drill. Place a ball on the green about 10 feet from the green's edge. From at least 30 feet away, try to putt another ball between the first ball and the fringe. Then try to get a third ball between the second ball and the fringe and so on. See how many balls you can putt before you run out of room or putting gets too difficult. Obviously, the closer you get each ball to the preceding one, the more successful you are.

The Yips

"I've got the yips" is perhaps the most feared phrase in golf. Any professional golfer with the yips may as well be on the green setting fire to dollar bills. Make that hundred dollar bills. Simply put, *yips* is a nervous condition that prevents the afflicted unfortunates from making any kind of smooth putting stroke. Instead, they are reduced to jerky little snatches at the ball, the putterhead seemingly possessing a mind all its own.

Some of the greatest players in the history of golf have had their careers — at least at the top level — cut short by the yips. Ben Hogan, perhaps the steeliest competitor ever, is one such player. His great rival, Sam Snead, is another. Arnold Palmer has a mild case. Bobby Jones, winner of the Grand Slam in 1930, had the yips. So did Tommy Armour, a brave man who lost an eye fighting in the trenches during World War I and then later won a British Open and a PGA Championship, but whose playing career was finished by his inability to hole short putts. Peter Alliss, a commentator on ABC Television, found that he couldn't even move the putter away from the ball toward the end of his career.

Perhaps the most famous recent example of someone getting the yips is two-time Masters winner Bernhard Langer, who has had the yips not once, not twice, but three times. To Langer's eternal credit, he has overcome the yips each time, hence his rather unique, homemade style where he seems to be taking his own pulse while over a putt.

Langer, who overcame the yips and is still considered one of the best putters in Europe, is the exception rather than the rule. As Henry Longhurst, the late, great writer and commentator, said about the yips, "Once you've had 'em, you've got 'em."

Longhurst, himself a yipper, once wrote a highly entertaining column on the yips, which opened with the following sentence: "There can be no more ludicrous sight than that of a grown man, a captain of industry, perhaps, and a pillar of his own community, convulsively jerking a piece of ironmongery to and fro in his efforts to hole a 3-foot putt." Longhurst is right, too. Pray that you don't get the yips.

So what causes this involuntary muscle-twitching over short putts? Mostly, I think it's fear of missing. Fear of embarrassment. Fear of who knows what. Whatever, it starts in the head. It can't be physical. After all, we're only talking about hitting the ball a short distance. What could be easier than that?

The yips spread insidiously through your body like a virus. When the yips reach your hands and arms, you're doomed. Your only recourse is a complete revamping of your method. Sam Snead started putting sidesaddle, facing the hole, holding his putter with a sort of split-handed grip, the ball to the right of his feet. Langer invented his own grip, as I've said. Other players have tried placing their left hand below the right on the putter. The long putter (described earlier in this chapter) has saved other players.

When Mac O'Grady did his study on the yips, he mailed 1,500 questionnaires to golfers everywhere. When the doctors at UCLA's Department of Neurology looked over the results, they told us that the only way to "fool" the yips is to stay ahead of them. When you do something long enough, like bending over to putt a certain way, your body is in what the doctors call a "length tension curve." This posture is recognized by the brain, and after you have missed putts for a long period of time, the subconscious takes over and starts to help by directing muscles to help get the ball into the hole. Your conscious and subconscious are fighting, and you're going to lose. So, without you knowing it, your right hand twitches, or your left forearm has spasms trying to help you get the ball into the hole. You're in full focal dystonia (involuntary spasms) right now, and that's not fun.

The remedy the doctors suggested was to change the length tension curve, or simply change the way you stand over a putt. The long putter surely makes you stand up to the ball differently, and maybe that's why those players always putt better immediately without the constraints of having the involuntary muscle movements known as the yips.

So if you get the yips, which usually comes with age, simply change something drastic in the way you set up the ball, make your grip totally different, or go bowling.

The real key, however, is getting over the notion that using any of those methods immediately identifies you as a yipper and in some way psychologically impaired. That, to my mind, is socially harsh. Don't be afraid to look different if you get the yips. Do whatever works.

The Art of Aiming the Ball

The golf swing is an assortment of trajectories flung around in time and space, with the golf club as the servant of the brain ill-equipped to do the directing in spatial darkness. Manifestations of your binocular acuity are the key to your pilgrimage. Are you in alignment with the parallel universe of focal obedience?
—Gary McCord, circa 1998, just after eating a lungfish tart

Golf is played with an assortment of physical skills and techniques. It is also played with the mind, which makes the final decisions and tells your motor system where and when things will happen, hopefully in some sort of dignified occurrence.

Some of the skills demanded by golf, and especially by putting, relate to peripheral vision, depth perception, binocularity (your eyes working as a team), eye-hand coordination, aiming accuracy, and visualization. These skills may well be more basic than grip, stance, and swing mechanics. I label this area *optics*.

The problem in golf is that what you perceive optically can be crystal clear yet inaccurate. And almost everything you *do* begins with what you see or perceive. Having to set up to the side of the ball and the target instead of behind them, as in other sports, really wreaks havoc with your optics. Trusting your optics in golf is like being in a house of mirrors, and you can be fooled easily. If your optical perception doesn't match reality, you see an illusion. (Me dating Cindy Crawford is an example.) And when your optics are tricked, you look at things like Mr. Magoo trying to read an eye chart — a little out of whack.

But you can be "re-educated" in optics. And right now, when you're first taking up the game, is a great time to start. A few simple exercises can make a world of difference as you start off on your quest to perfect putting. Putting doesn't involve a lot of mechanics, but it does require a whole bunch of perception.

Optics and alignment

Some say that the basis for a lot of what goes wrong out on the course is poor alignment, which often results from faulty optics. (I'll have to put this on my list of new excuses, right after solar flares.) When you miss a putt, you might blame your stroke, when really you may have missed because of improper alignment — a misperception of the target's location, the clubface as related to "square," or the green's characteristics.

Figure 3-14

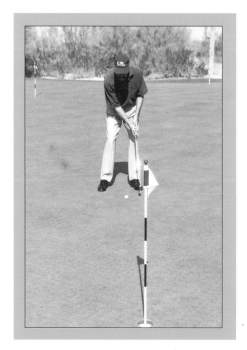

Nothing is more optically dependent than alignment. As I said earlier, the difficulty is that you have to deal with the surreal situation of being beside the target line rather than behind it — or do you?

You use two optical areas in determining your alignment: the address perspective and aim. The address perspective is your perspective when you stand next to the ball and assume your stance (see Figure 3-14). This is the more confusing area for most golfers. You use aim when you stare at the trash can, getting ready to throw a wadded-up piece of paper. You also use aim when you stand behind the ball and pick a line to putt on.

Some golfers use a spot a few feet in front of the ball when aiming. When they place their putters down behind the ball, they aim the face of the putter or the lines on the putter at that spot. Aligning to a spot a foot or so in front of the ball is easier than aligning to the hole, which may be several feet away.

Bowlers use this same kind of alignment strategy. If you've ever bowled, you know about the spots that are a few feet in front of you on the lane. You look at the spots and then pick a line to roll the ball over. After I discovered this technique in my bowling league, the Gutter Dwellers, my average rocketed to 87. (Check out my bowling technique in Figure 3-15.)

Figure 3-15

You can use a couple of other stategies to help with your alignment problems. The first one is to take the logo of the golf ball and set it along the line that you want the putt to follow. This can help you get a better visual reference to the line. Other players, like Tiger Woods, take a Sharpie pen and make a line about 1 inch in length on the ball (see Figure 3-16). You can use this method in the same way as the logo tip — to achieve a better visual reference for directing the ball down the intended path. When you stand over the putt, the ball is already aimed. That easy.

Figure 3-16

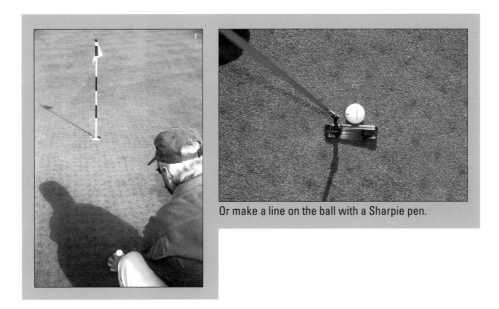

Or make a line on the ball with a Sharpie pen.

The eyes like lines

Players say that they putt better when they "see the line" of the putt. Some days when I play, the line is so visible that I can't miss. Unfortunately, this happens about once every presidential election year. Most of the time, I have to really concentrate to "see" the line. Another set of lines that can help improve your optics are the lines of your feet, knees, and shoulders. By keeping them square (at a right angle) to the target line, you aid your eyes in their appreciation of what is straight — and this helps keep your stroke on line.

To help you appreciate a clubface that's square to your target line, use tape or a yard-stick on the floor. Aim the tape at a distant target, such as your baby grand piano at the far end of your ballroom. Now set up at the end of the tape as if you were going to hit an imaginary ball straight down the tape line. You're practicing your visual alignment (which is a lot easier than practicing a 3-wood out of a fairway bunker with a large lip for three hours in a mild hailstorm). Give this drill a chance; it can really help you with your perception of straight lines.

When I'm having problems aligning my clubface, I take some of the gum that I've been chewing for the last three days and attach a tee to the putter with the fat end flush to the face, as shown in Figure 3-17. Then I aim that tee at the hole from about 3 feet away. (It's amazing how strong gum is after a three-day chew; in fact, I used it as mortar on my new brick mobile home.)

Figure 3-17

Your job is to stand there and visually appreciate what a square clubface looks like as you look down the attached tee to the hole. Spend a couple of minutes appreciating this perspective. If it looks okay to you on your first try, you're in line for your Bachelor of Alignment diploma. If not, repeat this drill daily until it looks okay the first time you place the club down. Use this drill to educate your eyes to a straight-line perspective and a square clubface.

Instant "preplay"

A rule of optics: When you have a mental picture of what you want to do, it often happens the way you picture it. How often have you dumped a shot into the water or a bunker and said, "I knew I was going to do that!" This is because you mentally perceived doom, and in your own clairvoyance you acted out the morbid scene. Stupid game.

To help overcome this problem in putting, I recommend watching others putt. Doing so trains you to optically appreciate the speed of the greens. Make a game of it. Guess how many seconds it will take for the ball to roll from the impact of the putter to its stopping point. Then time it — count one-thousand-one, one-thousand-two . . . , or use a stop watch or the second hand on your watch. Stay in the game, and always be aware of what's going on around you. Using these situations will help you play the game better.

As you observe others putting, notice that the ball goes through speed phases: the first being the fastest (acceleration), the second being sort of a glide, and the last being the slow-down-to-stop phase. Another reason to watch others putt is that, at first, you don't see the first several feet of the ball's roll because you're still fixated on the spot where the ball was.

Often, golfers tend to do this kind of optical preview when they stand aside the line, watching the ball roll off the putter. You say, "Pull a hamstring!" or "Grow hair!" if you hit a putt too hard and it is obviously going to zoom by the hole. You make the same type of comment — "Turn up the volume!" or "Get some enthusiasm!" — when the putt isn't going to get there. You make these comments (other than because you may be a little deranged) because you made an optical decision before you hit the ball. When the speed doesn't match the speed you imagined was necessary, you start spewing insults to the golf ball. (The funnier the insults, the more the ball tends to listen.)

After you get used to seeing what other players' putts look like, use this technique for your own putts. Look at the distance from the ball to the hole as if your eyes were walking the distance. Perhaps a 30-foot putt would take your eyes four seconds to look along the ground at a meaningful pace, while a 10-foot putt would take two seconds, and a 50-foot putt would take six seconds. Then take a practice stroke and imagine yourself hitting the ball at that speed, as shown in Figure 3-18.

I find this exercise very helpful when playing professionally. I spend some time on the practice putting green and get a feel for the speed of the greens. Then I incorporate "instant preplay," tracing the line with my eyes at the exact speed at which I think the ball will roll. Watch Phil Mickelson on television the next time he has a long putt. He assumes his address position and then traces the line with his eyes, tracking the line by using the "instant preplay" technique.

Figure 3-18

Speed kills

Almost every putt is what I call a "depth charge" launch. That means that it should have the speed to lurk around the hole and just maybe hit the hole and fall in. If you get it close, you might perform a burial with your balata. One of the best ways to develop a touch for the speed at which a putt should roll is to imagine things happening before they really do.

You must optically preview the putt's roll from its stationary point to a resting place near the hole — a tap-in is really nice. This optical preview activates the motor system to respond with the right amount of energy to hit the putt. You would use the same skill if I told you to throw a ball over a certain bush and make it land no more than 5 feet beyond the bush. All your actions use optics to determine at what arc and speed to toss the ball, and this information is relayed to the muscles.

Distance optics

Optical inaccuracy can cause an unwanted golf incident: the morbid three-putt. If there's any way to cut down on strokes, it is by eliminating extra putts. Statistics say that the average player has three to four three-putts per round — and for beginners, it's more like seven or eight. That's because you're often optically challenged when faced with long putts.

Most people perceive distances to be shorter than they actually are because of how the eyes triangulate (see Figure 3-19). You can gain this triangular perspective by holding one end of a string to your nose while the other end of the string is attached to a lazy uncle who has taken up residence on your couch for the last month.

Figure 3-19

The two eyes act as a team, pointing their visual axis at a target (your prone uncle). The angle of difference in convergence between the two eyes depends on how far away the target is — being more of an angle for a book 16 inches away and less of an angle for the wallowing blob on your couch. The lesser the angle, the farther away you perceive things to be. Unfortunately, even though you may think that your eyes are focused on the target, they may be focused on a point in front of the target, making you perceive the target to be closer than it really is.

This view is called "eyeballing" the distance. You look at the hole and expect to optically interpret the distance accurately. Wrong! But you can combat the optical distortion of a long putt in several ways:

✔ Use the "instant preplay" technique discussed earlier in this chapter.

✔ Stand beside the line like you're going to hit the putt. This is how your eyes are accustomed to viewing the landscape, and you can better judge the speed of the ball/greens in this position than if you stand directly behind the line.

✔ The more you improve the accuracy of the information your eyes and brain feed to your motor system, the more you can expect good results in the form of a putt that gets the ball close. This is a very good drill, and if I were you, I wouldn't go telling my friends about it.

✔ Look softly as you look at the hole from behind the ball, trying to expand your view to the sides of the hole. Doing so often improves your distance appreciation. (If you don't believe me, go back to the string exercise and instead of fixating on the end, open up your view.) Most often, expanding your peripheral vision helps you judge space.

✔ View the putt from a point off to the side and midway between the ball and the hole, as shown in Figure 3-20, rather than from behind the ball. Doing so may give you a better appreciation of the distance. Some players believe that, from this position, they can better visualize the speed necessary for the putt.

Figure 3-20

Optics and reading greens

Poor green reading is the number-one culprit for golfers; they just don't do it as well as they could or should. One reason is that greens are the most diabolically devilish form of fun that a course architect has.

Greens cause the balls to curve right, left, and sometimes both ways — a dual existence of fun and frolic. Even the pros know that reading greens is visual mayhem and that if they can minimize their misreads, they will make more putts and experience the sweet nectar of cash flow.

Optics are important in green reading, and here's why: It's all in the eyes of the beholder. Those demonic course designers are very sure of the ways they can create visual chaos. For example, it's common to make snap judgments as you approach a green. When your eyes look at all greens from several yards in front, they look like they slope from back to front. Many of the old, pre-1950 courses have this design, which drains the greens so that water doesn't collect on the putting surfaces and rot the grass.

If the green does slope from back to front, to keep things simple, all putts break toward the fairway. A putt that is hit from the left side of the green to the center or the right generally breaks toward the fairway. The same goes for a putt hit from the right side of the green to the center or the left side.

How much break is the key here. The only way to tell is to look from the best optical perspective — to assess the green from the side. For a putt going from back to front or vice versa, this is the best position from which to optically assess the slope — uphill, downhill, or level. Don't worry if at first it's hard to tell how much higher the back of the green is than the front. Keep looking for these subtleties. Your optics will improve as you become more observant.

Looking behind the ball or behind the hole is the best way to tell optically whether the putt is straight or breaks right or left. One of the smartest things you can do is to arrange a green-reading tour with your local golf course professional. Look at this as a field trip to an outdoor library, and take some sunscreen.

A good general rule: Don't change your mind about your stroke strategy while over a putt. First, things look different from here than from the side! Second, the ground you stand on may not be sloped the same as it is up by the hole. And because of the speed of the putt, unless it is all downhill, the ball will travel too fast over the slope near it and break only near the middle to the last third of the putt. (Another reason to stand to the side of the putt — it's easier to assess the last third of the putt from this position.)

Some things you may want to write down in your reminder book:

✔ Fast greens break more, so don't hit the ball too hard. But keep in mind that hitting the ball more softly means that the slope will affect it more.

✔ Downhill putts act like fast greens, as the roll of the ball to the hole is affected by the slope for more than the last few feet.

✔ Slow greens break less, so you must hit the ball harder. That initial burst of speed prevents the ball from breaking as much.

✔ Uphill putts act like slow greens. Your challenge is to figure out how much uphill slope you're dealing with, and then adjust your putt accordingly — the more slope, the more power it takes, or the farther back you imagine the hole from where it really is.

Points of the roll

I gave you a lot on information on some complicated stuff relating to optics and alignment, so here's a summary of the points that were made:

✔ Keep your alignment parallel to the target line.

- Feet

- Knees

- Shoulders

- Eye line

✔ Know what your putter blade looks like square to the line.

✔ Follow the line of your intended putt with your eyes at the speed that you think the ball will roll.

✔ Stare at the line of your putt longer than you look at the golf ball.

✔ Use the logo line or a line that you have marked on the golf ball to help you align your putts.

You start off not housebroken in relation to putting. You have to be trained. It takes practice. The boys at the club practice putting less than anything else, and putting can take up more than half the strokes you play in this silly game. Create some games on the putting green to enhance your desire to go there.

Chapter 4

Chipping and Pitching

In This Chapter

▸ Understanding what the short game is

▸ Realizing the importance of the short game

▸ Chipping your way to success

▸ Pitching yourself out of a tight spot

*F*ive-time PGA champion Walter Hagen had the right attitude. He stood Fon the first tee knowing that he would probably hit at least six terrible shots that day. So when he did hit terrible shots, he didn't get upset. Hagen simply relied on his superior short game (every shot within 80 yards of the hole) to get him out of trouble. That combination of attitude and dexterity made him a fearsome match player. His apparent nonchalance — "Always take time to smell the flowers," he used to say — and his ability to get up and down "from the garbage" put a lot of pressure on his opponents. His opponents became depressed or annoyed and eventually downhearted. More often than not, Hagen won his matches without having hit his full shots too solidly. Golf is more than hitting the ball well. Golf is a game of managing your misses.

Say you have a strong long game relative to your short game prowess. What's probably going to happen is that your range of scores isn't going to be that large. Your high scores will probably be only about six shots higher than your low ones. Now, you probably think that's pretty good, and it is. But it's a two-sided coin. While your long game may give you consistency, your short game takes away your ability to capitalize on it in the form of some really low scores.

Golf Has Its Ups and Downs

As I mentioned earlier, the short game is every shot hit within 80 yards of the hole. That includes sand play (which I cover in Chapter 5) and putting (which I cover in Chapter 3). But they have chapters of their own. So what's left? Chipping and pitching — two versions of short shots to the green, pitching being the higher flier.

Hang around golfers for only a short while, and you inevitably hear one say something along the lines of, "I missed the third green to the right but got up and down for my par." At this stage, you're probably wondering what in the world "up and down" means. Well, the "up" part is the subject of this chapter — chipping or pitching the ball to the hole. The "down" half of the equation, of course, is holing the putt after your chip or pitch (see Chapter 3). Thus a golfer with a good short game is one who gets "up and down" a high percentage of the time (anywhere above 50 percent).

The weird thing is that, although a good short game is where you can retrieve your mistakes and keep a good score going, a lot of amateurs tend to look down on those blessed with a delicate touch around the greens. They hate to lose to someone who beats them with good chipping and putting. Somehow a strong short game isn't perceived as "macho golf" — at least not in the same way as smashing drives 300 yards and hitting low, raking iron shots to greens is macho. Good ball strikers tend to look down on those players with better short games. This attitude is a snobbery thing. It's also a missing-the-point thing.

TIP

In golf, you want to get the ball around the course while achieving the lowest score you can. How you get that job done is up to you. No rule says that you have to look pretty when you play golf. Your round isn't going to be hung in an art gallery. As someone once said, "Three of them and one of those makes four." Remember that saying. You can rescue a lot of bad play with one good putt.

You don't hear today's professionals downplaying the importance of a good short game. Professionals know that the short game is where they make their money. Here's proof: If you put a scratch (zero) handicap amateur and a tournament pro on the tee with drivers in their hands, the two shots don't look that much different. Sure, you can tell who is the better player, but the amateur at least looks competitive.

The gap in quality grows on the approach shots, again on wedge play, and then again on the short game. In fact, the closer the players get to the green, the more obvious the difference in level of play. On the green is where a mediocre score gets turned into a good score and where a good score gets turned into a great score. (Take a look at the sample scorecard in Figure 4-1. It probably wouldn't hurt to keep this kind of record for yourself once in a while.)

Figure 4-1

Men's Course Rating/Slope — Blue 73.1/137, White 71.0/130
Women's Course Rating/Slope — Red 73.7/128

Blue Tees	White Tees	Par	Hcp	JOHN				HOLE	HIT FAIRWAY	HIT GREEN	NO. PUTTS	Hcp	Par	Red Tees
377	361	4	11	4				1	✓	✓	2	13	4	310
514	467	5	13	8				2	✓	0	3	3	5	428
446	423	4	1	7				3	0	0	2	1	4	389
376	356	4	5	6				4	0	0	2	11	4	325
362	344	4	7	5				5	0	✓	3	7	4	316
376	360	4	9	6				6	✓	0	2	9	4	335
166	130	3	17	4				7	0	✓	3	17	3	108
429	407	4	3	5				8	✓	✓	3	5	4	368
161	145	3	15	5				9	0	0	2	15	3	122
3207	2993	35		50				Out	4	4	22		35	2701
		Initial										Initial		
366	348	4	18	5				10	0	0	2	14	4	320
570	537	5	10	7				11	✓	0	3	2	5	504
438	420	4	2	5				12	✓	0	2	6	4	389
197	182	3	12	4				13	0	0	2	16	3	145
507	475	5	14	5				14	✓	✓	2	4	5	425
398	380	4	4	5				15	0	✓	3	8	4	350
380	366	4	6	5				16	✓	0	2	10	4	339
165	151	3	16	4				17	0	0	2	18	3	133
397	375	4	8	5				18	0	0	2	12	4	341
3418	3234	36		45				In	3	2	20		36	2946
6625	6227	71		95				Tot	7	6	42		71	5647
Handicap												Handicap		
Net Score												Net Score		
Adjust												Adjust		

Scorer   Attested   Date

Okay, I've convinced you of the importance of the short game in the overall scheme of things. Before you go any further, you need to know the difference between a chip and a pitch. In the United States, this question is easy to answer. A *chip* is a short shot that's mostly on the ground. A *pitch*, in contrast, is generally a longer shot that's mostly in the air.

Golf gets a bit more complicated in a country like Scotland. In Scotland, the game of golf is played with the ball more on the ground. The climate is generally colder and windier and the turf firmer, so hitting low shots makes more sense and is more effective, given the conditions. As a result, the contrast between a chip and a pitch is a little more blurred. In Scotland, golfers hit what they call *pitch and runs*, where the ball spends a fair amount of time in the air and then the same amount of time on the ground. Especially in the summer, when the ground is hard, Scottish players cannot land shots directly on the putting surface. So the bounce and roll of the ball becomes a bigger part of the shot.

Having made that qualification, thinking of chipping and pitching in the "American" way is a lot simpler.

A Chip Off the Old Block

Chips are short shots played around the greens with anything from a 5-iron to a sand wedge. The basic idea is to get the ball on the green and rolling as fast as you can. If you get the ball running like a putt, judging how far it will go is a lot easier.

Points of reference

Your first point of reference is the spot where you want the ball to land. If at all possible, you want that spot to be on the putting surface. The putting surface's turf is generally flatter and better prepared and makes the all-important first bounce more predictable. You want to avoid landing chips on rough, uneven, or sloping ground.

Pick a spot about 2 feet onto the green (see Figure 4-2). From that spot, I visualize the ball running along the ground toward the hole. Visualization is a big part of chipping. Try to see the shot in your mind's eye before you hit the ball. Then be as exact as you can with your target. You can't be too precise.

Figure 4-2

Which club to use

You determine which club to use by the amount of room you have between your landing point and the hole. If you only have 15 feet, you need to use a more lofted club (one with a face that is severely angled back from vertical), like a sand wedge so that the ball doesn't run too far.

If you've ever watched golf on TV, you've probably seen Phil Mickelson use a full swing to hit the ball straight up in the air and cover only a short distance on the ground. Phil can do another thing that is really astounding. You stand about 6 feet away from Phil and turn your back to him. You then cup your hands and hold them out from your chest. Phil takes a full swing with his sand wedge and lofts the ball over your head and into your sweaty, waiting hands — all from only 6 feet away. Now that's a lob wedge!

If that gap is a lot bigger — say, 60 feet — then a straighter-faced club, like a 7-iron, is more practical. Figure 4-3 illustrates this concept.

Figure 4-3

From address...

think where you want the ball to land...

then try to hit it...

so that the ball runs to the hole.

The problem of lie

Then you have the problem of how the ball is lying on the ground. When the ball is in longer grass, you need to use a more lofted club and make a longer swing (longer grass means a longer swing), no matter where the hole is. You need to get the ball high enough to escape the longer rough. If the ball is lying "down" in a depression and you can't get the ball out with the straight-faced club, which the situation normally calls for, you have to go to more loft and move the ball back in your stance (closer to your right foot) a little to make the shot work. So this part of the game does require flexibility.

Use the philosophy that I've outlined as a starting point, not as a holy writ that must be followed to the letter. Let your own creativity take over. Go with your instincts when you need to choose the right club or shot. The more you practice this part of your game, the better your instincts become.

Practice, and only practice, makes you better. Try all sorts of clubs for these shots. Sooner or later, you'll develop a feel for the shots. I stress that you should use as many clubs as possible when practicing. Using different clubs helps you work on the technique and not the shot.

How to hit a chip

Short game guru Phil Rodgers taught me my chipping technique, which is basically the same one that I employ for putting. I use a putting stroke, but with a lofted club. And I want you to do the same. Take your putting grip and stroke — and go hit chip shots.

The key to chipping is the setup. Creating the right positions at address is essential.

You want your stance to be narrow, about 12 inches from heel to heel, and open — pull your left foot back from the target line. Your shoulders should be open to the target as well. Then place about 80 percent of your weight on your left side. By moving your hands ahead of the ball, you encourage the downward strike that you need to make solid contact with the ball. Place the ball on a line about 2 inches to the left of your right big toe, as shown in Figure 4-4.

Figure 4-4

During your stroke, focus on the back of your left wrist. Your left wrist must stay flat and firm, as in putting (see Figure 4-5). To keep your wrist flat, tape a Popsicle stick to the back of your wrist (between your wrist and your watch works almost as well). You feel any breakdowns right away. Now go hit some putts and chips.

Figure 4-5

Put a pen inside your watchband.

That'll firm up your wrist.

When I play a tour event, one of the first things I do is go to the putting green and hit some putts/chips to get an idea of the speed of the greens. I get a flat spot in the green and take some golf balls off the green by 5 feet. I then put a coin down on the green 2 feet from the fringe (the fringe is a collar of grass, which is longer than the grass on the green but shorter than the grass on the fairway, that surrounds the green). Then I take an 8, 9, and wedge from the spot off the green and chip balls onto the green, trying to bounce each ball off the coin and letting it then run to the hole. I get a real good idea of how fast the greens are that week. You can also develop a touch for those shots — and when you miss as many greens as I do, the practice comes in real handy.

Make Your Pitch

Pitch shots, which you play only with your wedges and 9-iron, are generally longer than chip shots, so, as you'd expect, you need to make a longer swing, which introduces wrist action into the equation. Which introduces the problem of how long your swing should be and how fast. In other words, pitch shots need some serious feel.

Even the best players try to avoid pitch shots. They are "in-between" shots. You can't just make your normal, everyday full swing — that would send the ball way too far. You're stuck making a half-type swing. A half-type swing is never easy, especially when you're under pressure.

Anyway, here's how to build your pitching swing.

First, adopt the same stance that you did for the chip shot: same width, same posture, same ball position. The only difference is in the alignment of your shoulders, which should be parallel to your toe line, open to the target line, as shown in Figure 4-6.

Figure 4-6

When you pitch, your shoulders and feet must be aligned to the left of where you want the ball to go.

Now make a mini-swing (which I describe in Chapter 1). Without moving the butt end of the club too far in your backswing, hinge your wrists so that the shaft is horizontal. Then swing through the shot. Watch how far the ball goes. That distance is your point of reference. You want to hit the next pitch 10 yards farther? Make your swing a little longer (see Figure 4-7). Shorter? Your swing follows suit. That way, your rhythm never changes. You want the clubhead accelerating smoothly through the ball. And that acceleration is best achieved if the momentum is built up gradually from address.

Poor pitchers of the ball do one of two things: Either they start their swings way too slowly and then have to speed up too much at impact, or they jerk the club away from the ball and have to decelerate later. Both swings lead to what golf columnist Peter Dobereiner christened "sickening knee-high fizzers" — low, thin shots that hurtle uncontrollably over the green, or complete duffs that travel only a few feet. Not a pretty sight. The cause of both is often tension. Relax. Imagine that you're swinging with a potato chip between your teeth. Focus on not biting down on it. That'll keep you relaxed.

Here's a game we play at the back of the range at our facility at Grayhawk Golf Course in Scottsdale, Arizona. We get five empty buckets and place them in a straight line at 20, 40, 60, 80, and 100 feet. We then have one hour to hit one ball in each bucket, starting at 20 feet. The winner gets the title to the other guy's car. We're still driving our own cars; we usually get frustrated and quit before the one hour time limit expires or we go to lunch, but we get some good practice pitching the ball.

Remember, in golf, you get better by doing; you don't get better by doing nothing.

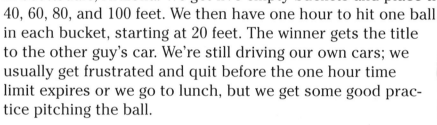

Last pitching thought: Although pitch shots fly higher than chips, apply the same philosophy to your pitching. Get the ball on the ground as soon as possible. Pick out your landing area and let the ball roll. See the shot in your mind's eye before you hit the ball, and remember your *Golf For Dummies* secret: Hit down; don't lift the ball.

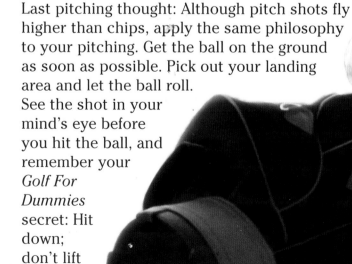

Figure 4-7

From address…

swing the club with hands/arms only…

accelerate through impact to a relaxed finish.

Chapter 5
· · · · · · · ·
It's Your Sandbox:
Sand Play

The 5th Wave   By Rich Tennant

"What exactly do the rules say about giving and receiving advice?"

In This Chapter

· ·

▸ What is a bunker?

▸ Understanding sand play

▸ Achieving a sound sand technique

▸ Dealing with a less-than-perfect lie

· ·

*I*have read countless articles and books on sand play, and they all say the same thing: Because you don't even have to hit the ball, playing from the sand is the easiest part of golf. Bull trap! If sand play were the easiest aspect of the game, all those articles and books would have no reason to be written in the first place. Everyone would be blasting the ball onto the putting surface with nary a care in the world. And that, take it from me, is certainly not the case.

Bunkers: Don't Call 'Em Sand Traps!

Bunkers, or sand traps (as I am told not to call them on television), provoke an extraordinary amount of "sand angst" among golfers. But sometimes, *aiming* for a bunker actually makes sense — on a long, difficult approach shot, for example. The pros know that the "up and down" from sand (see Chapter 3) can actually be easier than from the surrounding (usually long and thick) grass.

Bunkers began life as holes in the ground on the windswept Scottish linksland. Because the holes were sheltered from the cold breezes, sheep would take refuge in them. Thus the holes expanded. When the land came to be used for golf, the locals took advantage of what God and the sheep left and fashioned sand-filled bunkers from the holes. (No word on what the sheep thought of all this.)

On these old courses, the greens were sited so as to maximize the bunker's threat to golfers' shots, which is why they came to be named "hazards" in the rules of golf. Later, course architects would place these insidious "traps" so as to penalize wayward shots. That's why you generally don't see bunkers in the middle of fairways — they're mostly to the sides.

As for how much sand you find in a typical bunker, that varies. I prefer a depth of about 2 inches. That stops balls from burying too much on landing but still provides a decent cushion for the escape shot.

I don't know too many amateurs who have ever aimed at a bunker. Mired in a bunker is the last place they want to finish. Typifying the way in which amateur golfers look at bunkers is the experience the late Tip O'Neill had a few years ago during the first few days of the Bob Hope Chrysler Classic, which is a Pro-Am tournament. The former Speaker of the House, admittedly not the strongest golfer (even among celebrities), found himself in a very deep bunker. He then spent the next few hours (okay, the time just seemed that long) trying to extricate first the ball, and then himself, from the trap — all on national television. You could almost hear the millions of viewers saying to themselves, "Yeah, been there, done that."

Well, they haven't really done that from this bunker. The bunker that poor Tip O'Neill was trying to extricate himself from is the deepest pit I've seen since my financial situation in the 1980s. This greenside bunker is located on the 16th hole at PGA West Stadium Golf Course in LaQuinta, California. The bunker is so deep that you can't walk straight up out of it; a path goes diagonally up the hill, and the famous Himalayan mountain guides, the Sherpas, lead the way. I did a video on this course back in the late '80s. We used a helicopter, which started on the bunker floor and rose up to the green as my ball was blasted from this insidious hole with the cameras rolling. Gosh, I love show business.

Why is that, though? Why is it that most amateurs are scared to death every time their shots end up in a greenside bunker? Just what is it about sand play that they find so tough? Well, after much research, some of it in a laboratory, I've come to the conclusion the problem is simple. (If it weren't simple, I would never have discovered it.) It all comes down to lack of technique and/or a lack of understanding.

Faced with a bunker shot, many golfers are beaten before they start. You can tell by their constipated looks, sweaty foreheads, and hesitant body language. Their reaction when they fail is also interesting. After a couple of shots finish up back in the bunker, most people don't focus on their technique. They merely try to hit the shot harder, making more and more violent swings. Not good. Hitting the ball harder only makes them angrier than before because the ball sure isn't going to come out. Still, they finish with a nice big hole, which is perfect if they want to bury a small pet but not much good for anything else.

Practice only helps

Getting the ball out of a bunker can be very easy after you practice enough and get a feel for it. I knew at an early age that my scoring depended on getting up and down out of the bunkers with a certain regularity, so I practiced bunkers with a vengeance. As a result, I can get a ball out of a bunker with everything from a sand wedge to a putter.

One day I was playing in the Kemper Open in Charlotte, North Carolina, when I saw a notoriously bad bunker player who was on the tour practicing hard on his sand play. After a few moments of idle conversation and general harassing, a bet transpired. He would hit ten balls with his sand wedge; I would hit five balls with a putter. If I got my ball closer than his ball, he would have to go in the locker room and announce to everyone that I beat him with a putter out of a bunker. If he won, I would take him to dinner and then not bother him for the rest of the year.

The laughter from the locker room echoed throughout the clubhouse, and his reputation as the worst bunker player on tour remained intact. I cannot divulge his name because he is playing the senior tour now and is doing very well. He got much better getting out of the sand after some needed practice.

Part of the reason for this all-too-human reaction is that long stretches of failure resign you to your fate. In your mind, you've tried everything, and you still can't get the damn thing out. So you trudge into the bunker expecting the worst, and you usually get it.

The Problem with Sand Play

A huge majority of golfers stand to the ball in a way that makes it all but impossible for them to create the correct angles in their golf swing. Golf, and especially bunker play, is only the creation of the proper angle that the clubhead must take into the ball. Sometimes, the root of the many duffs, hacks, slashes, and any other sort of poor shot is ball position. If you have the ball positioned way back toward your right foot, as so many people seem to do, you won't ever get the ball out of the trap. You can't hit the ball high enough, for one thing. For another, the clubhead enters the sand at too steep an angle. In other words, the clubhead digs into the sand instead of sliding through it. When that happens, the ball usually remains in the bunker sucking sand.

And that's what I mean by a lack of understanding. Poor bunker players get into the sand and start "digging" as if they are having a day out at a quarantined beach. Sometimes I feel like throwing poor bunker players a bucket and shovel so that they can dig for clams. Then at least they'd have something to show for all their efforts.

To Be — Or Not to Be — Handy from Sand

To be a competent sand player, you must take advantage of the way your sand wedge is designed. The bottom of the club can have a different width (see Figure 5-1). The bounce is the bottom of the clubhead — the part that, when you hold the club in front of your face, hangs below the leading edge. Believe me, if you can make the best use of the bounce, bunker play will be taken off your endangered species list.

The bounce is the part of the clubhead that should contact the sand first. Doing so encourages the sliding motion that's so crucial to good bunker play. Think about it. The sand is going to slow the club as you swing down and through, which is okay. But you want to keep the slowdown to a minimum. If the club digs in too much, it will also slow down too much. If that happens, the ball probably won't get out of the bunker. So slide the clubhead; don't use it to "dig." Take note, however, that not every sand wedge is equipped with the same amount of bounce. The width of the sole and the amount that it hangs below the leading edge varies. This, of course, begs another question: How do you know how much bounce your sand wedge needs? The determining factor is the type of sand you play from. The bigger the bounce or the wider the sole on your sand wedge, the less it will dig into the sand.

Figure 5-1

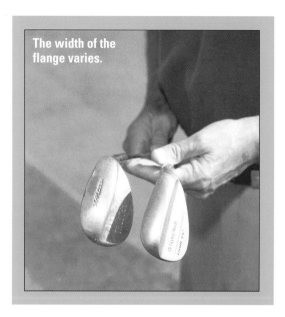

The width of the flange varies.

If the sand at your home club is typically pretty firm underfoot, to be most effective, you need to use a sand wedge with very little bounce. A club with a lot of bounce does just that — bounce. And hard (or wet) sand only accentuates that tendency. So using that club is only going to see you hitting a lot of shots thin, the clubhead skidding off the sand and contacting the ball's equator. Either you hit the ball into the face of the bunker and don't get out at all, or the ball misses the face and finishes way over the green. Neither result is socially acceptable.

At the other end of the scale is really soft, deep sand. For that sort of stuff, you need a lot of bounce. In fact, because the clubhead digs so easily when the sand is soft, you can't have enough bounce.

Anyway, enough of this preamble. Take a look at how a sound sand technique is properly — and easily — achieved.

GARY SAYS

"Hoe-ly cow!"

Once, while in Vail, Colorado, I received an urgent phone call from director Ron Shelton while he was shooting the movie *Tin Cup*. He said, "Gary, we forgot to ask you this, but how do you hit a gardening hoe out of a bunker?" "Gee, Ron," I said, "I haven't done that in a while; let me think. What do you mean, how do you hit a gardening hoe out of a bunker?" Ron told me that a scene had to be taken the next day with Kevin Costner hitting a shot out of a bunker, with a hoe, and that the ball had to land no more than 3 feet from the hole. Sure. Right.

I went to the practice green at Singletree Golf Course with my shag bag full of balls and a hoe. It was pouring down rain. It took me at least 40 minutes to get a single ball out of the bunker,

and I *bladed* (hit the center of the ball with the leading edge) that one to get it out. I finally decided that the bottom edge of the hoe was too sharp and I needed some bounce to make it perform better in the sand. So I bent the hoe on the bottom and immediately started to get the ball up and out.

I called the movie set and gave directions on the technique of how to bend the hoe. I saw the film three days later, and Kevin Costner hit the first ball 3 feet out of the bunker, with the hoe, to 2 feet. That's a take; wrap it up, as they say. So if the bounce can work to get a ball out of a bunker with a hoe, think what it can do for your sand wedge.

The Splash

Okay, you're in a greenside bunker. You want to get the ball out and onto the putting surface in fewer than two shots. Here's what to do: Open your stance by pulling your left foot back. Pull your foot back until you start to feel vaguely ridiculous. Your left foot's position must feel funny to you. If it doesn't, pull your foot back more. Next, open (turn to the right) your sand wedge to the point where the face is almost looking straight up at the sky, as shown in Figure 5-2. The ball should be positioned forward in your stance toward your left heel. (Do this even more if you're unlucky enough to finish very close to the face of the bunker.) You should feel like you'll go right under the ball when you swing at it. This position should feel just as weird as your stance. Again, if it doesn't, turn your sand wedge to the right even more.

Figure 5-2

Your hands should be "behind" the ball.

At address, pull your left foot back.

Turn the clubface clockwise until it looks skyward.

Most amateurs I play with don't do either of those things. They stand too square and don't open the clubface nearly enough (see Figure 5-3). In effect, they don't take advantage of their sand wedges. This club is most efficient when the face is wide open (turned clockwise). Sand wedges are designed that way. The open face sends the ball up when you hit the sand.

Figure 5-3

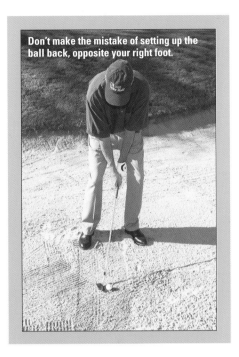

Don't make the mistake of setting up the ball back, opposite your right foot.

Here's one other thing that you should be aware of. When I go home to play, I notice that nobody practices bunker shots, not even my pal "sand wedge Sam." (He got his nickname after demonstrating an uncommon prowess in the much underestimated and neglected art of sand wedge tossing.) Don't fall into that trap (I love bad puns); get into a bunker and practice. Besides, you never know, you may like bunkers.

Finally, remember that your club must not touch the sand before you hit the ball.

Okay, you're over the shot, now what? You want to know where to hit the sand, right?

Aim to hit the sand about a credit card length behind the ball. Swing at about 80 percent of full speed. Think of it as a sliding motion. Don't hit down. Let the clubhead throw a "scoop" of sand onto the green, as shown in Figure 5-4. Focusing on a full, uninhibited follow-through will help you (see Figure 5-5). Forget the ball. All you're trying to do is throw sand out of the bunker. (The more sand you throw, the shorter the shot will be. So if you need to hit the shot a fair distance, hit maybe only 2 inches behind the ball.) If you can throw sand, the ball will be carried along for the ride. And that's why better players say that bunker play is easy — the clubhead never actually contacts the ball. Now go get some sunblock and spend some time practicing in the sand.

Figure 5-4

Try to slide the clubhead under the ball... throwing some sand and the ball onto the green.

Figure 5-5

Make a full follow-through. Recock your wrist right after impact.

Buried Alive!

Unfortunately, not every lie (where the ball is sitting) in a bunker is perfect. Sometimes the ball *plugs* — embeds itself in the sand so that only part of it is visible. You'll hear other golfers describe this sort of lie as a *fried egg*. When that happens to your ball, and after you're through cursing your bad luck, you need to employ a different technique.

Or at least a different alignment of the clubface. You still need your open stance, but this time don't open the clubface. Keep it a little *hooded*. In other words, align the club-face to the left of your ultimate target. Now, shift nearly all your weight to your left side, which puts you "ahead" of the shot (see Figure 5-6). Also, the ball should be played back in your stance. This is the one time that you want the leading edge of the club to *dig*. The ball, after all, is below the surface.

Figure 5-6

Put the ball back in your stance...

but don't change your posture.

Close the clubface at address.

Okay, you're ready. Swing the club up and down, and I mean up and down like you're chopping wood with a dull ax. Hit straight down on the sand a couple of inches behind the ball (see Figure 5-7). A follow-through isn't needed. Just hit down. Hard. The ball should pop up and then run to the hole. Because no backspin is on the golf ball, the ball will run like it just stole something. So allow for it.

Just how hard you should hit down is hard for me to say because it depends on the texture and depth of the sand and on how deep the ball is buried. That old standby, practice, tells you all that you need to know.

Second-to-last point: Experiment with different lofted clubs, and then use whatever works. Many times I use my pitching wedge (which has little bounce and a sharper leading edge and, therefore, digs more) with this technique.

Last point: Always smooth out your footprints when leaving a bunker. If a rake isn't lying nearby, use your feet.

Or if you're like my buddy Steamroller Ron, just roll around in the bunker until it's real smooth. Groups used to gather to watch Ron smooth out the sand. We had very few rakes at the Muni, and the Steamroller was the nearest thing we had to one. I miss Steamroller; he sold his gravel business and moved to Saudi Arabia.

Figure 5-7

"Bury" the club in the sand... which shortens your follow-through.